THE EXTRA MILE

One

Woman's

Personal

Journey

to

Ultrarunning

Greatness

RODALE

Notice

Mention of specific companies, organizations, or authorities in this book does not imply endorsement by the author or publisher, nor does mention of specific companies, organizations, or authorities imply that they endorse this book, its author, or the publisher.

© 2006 by Pam Reed

Rodale books may be purchased for promotional use or for special sales. For information, please write to: Special Markets Department, Rodale Inc., 733 Third Avenue, New York, NY 10017.

Printed in the United States of America

Rodale Inc. makes every effort to use acid-free ♾, recycled paper ♻.

Book design by Gavin Robinson

All Badwater photographs are by Dave Nelson. All other photographs appearing in this book are from the personal collection of Pam Reed.

Library of Congress Cataloging-in-Publication Data

Reed, Pam.
    The extra mile : one woman's personal journey to ultrarunning greatness / Pam Reed.
        p.   cm.
    ISBN-13 978-1-59486-415-5   hardcover
    ISBN-10 1-59486-415-2   hardcover
    ISBN-13 978-1-59486-730-9   paperback
    ISBN-10 1-59486-730-5   paperback
    1. Reed, Pam.   2. Runners (Sports)—United States—Biography.   3. Women runners—United States—Biography.   I. Title.
    GV1061.15.R42A3   2006
    796.42092—dc22
    [B]   2006011787

Distributed to the trade by Holtzbrinck Publishers

2   4   6   8   10   9   7   5   3   1   hardcover

    6   8   10   9   7   paperback

RODALE
LIVE YOUR WHOLE LIFE™

We inspire and enable people to improve their lives and the world around them

For more of our products visit rodalestore.com or call 800-848-4735

I want to dedicate this book to my husband, Jim, and my kids.

First, this is for Jim—if it wasn't for him I wouldn't even have tried ultrarunning. I also wouldn't be director of the Tucson Marathon. Those were both Jim's ideas, and I just ran with them. He has made a lot of sacrifices for me and for our family. He really is one of the hardest-working and most energetic people I know.

My kids, Timothy, Andrew, and Jackson, have had many times when their mother has not been around. I hope that they can see that through hard work you can accomplish just about anything. All three of my kids are really good people. I can't wait to see what neat things they will do when they grow up.

I want to dedicate this book to my husband, Jim, and my kids.

CONTENTS

ONE: WHERE I STARTED

TWO: WHERE I AM

CONTENTS

THREE: WHERE I'M GOING

FOREWORD

BY CHARLIE ENGLE

Inspiration and guidance are often sought in the pages of books, and on rare occasions a volume will generously reward the reader with a sense of comfort and direction. On the surface, Pam Reed's accomplishments would seem to be anything but comfortable. And Pam really only knows how to move in one direction: *forward*. So where does that leave the reader of these words? On the edge of his or her seat, anxious to find out what happens next. Ultimately, though, the reader will be comforted and inspired by Pam's matter-of-fact approach to running and to life.

Pam Reed's story is important for many reasons that have absolutely nothing to do with running. She has proven time and again that gender, age, and physical stature are minor factors when compared with determination and sheer will. In a world where many mothers use having a family as an excuse to quit exercising, Pam is driven to show that being married and the mother of three boys (stepmom to two more) is a reason to *start* running. She understands that the best way to inspire one's children is by being a good example. Don't just *tell* them what to do, *show* them.

Does Pam Reed have an ego? You bet she does. Does she enjoy winning and setting records? Of course. But winning and records are not enough to explain Pam's drive and determination. This book gives some insight into the intangible personality traits that push Pam beyond her own physical limitations.

I met Pam several years ago at a prerace party for Badwater, the 135-mile Death Valley ultramarathon. She was the defending champion and I was a race rookie. I watched her from a distance as she mingled with other runners, and I was struck by a very specific thought: *She doesn't want to be here!* By *here*, I meant at that party. She would have much preferred to be running. At that moment, I realized that she was very much like me—insecure, uncertain, driven. Outwardly confident, yet tormented by doubts. I liked her. Ultimately she won her second straight Badwater and I barely survived.

Two years later, in 2005, I was back to try again and so was Pam. I was very anxious and hoped to finish the race without needing any serious medical attention. I started with Pam and about 25 other runners at 10:00 a.m. I used Pam as my gauge for pacing myself. In 2003, I was well ahead of Pam for much of the race and then fell apart while she went on to win. This time I decided that I would stay behind her. It turned out to be a smart decision on my part. My first 50 miles were very strong and I was feeling good. Only a big mistake on my part would stop me from doing well. That mistake came at about 52 miles, when I took off my hat. Sometimes runners in extreme conditions do stupid things. For some unknown reason, I removed my hat, exposing my head to temperatures well over 120 degrees. At about the 57-mile mark, I began to overheat. At the 58-mile mark, I passed Pam and her crew. Pam is very competitive and I am sure she did not like seeing me go past her. So what did she do? She told me to put my hat back on, giving me a brief but poignant lecture about keeping cool. She probably saved my race. I went on to finish a surprising third that year, actually beating Pam for the first time in any race. She didn't have to help me, but she did.

To a lot of people, ultrarunning doesn't make sense. I can't explain why someone like Pam Reed does what she does. She can give lots of reasons for it, but even she can't identify that part of her that forces her to keep moving forward, searching for the next life lesson. That is one of the things that make her special. Oh, and one word of advice to the reader: You might as well put on your running shoes now, because you will be running down a trail soon.

PROLOGUE:
BOSTON OR BUST

It was 1996, the 100th running of the Boston Marathon, and I was all set to go! For long-distance runners, there's something absolutely unique about Boston. Thousands of athletes from all over the world first have to qualify for and then make their way to the mother of all marathons—and I would be among them. I was still relatively new to distance running, and I was really psyched to take part in the 100th running of the event.

But for me, getting into the race—accomplished by running a qualifying time at a qualifying marathon elsewhere during the year before the Boston—was not a foregone conclusion. In 1995, I was pregnant with my third son, Jackson, and while it's true that I ran all through my pregnancy, I was not running long races.

Jackson made his appearance in the world on July 23. It probably goes without saying that just after giving birth you're not really in peak condition. Jackson's delivery had been a cesarean section, which I somehow didn't think of as major surgery. I then had to get ready for Boston because my last chance to qualify would be in Chicago in October. So, just to give myself a gentle workout, in late September I entered a 100-mile race, the Angeles Crest near Los Angeles. A friend of mine had told me about this race—he'd crewed it before and told me that it was a fun course.

Well, that wasn't my experience. By mile 50 my quads were shot. I was in so much pain that I started yelling at my friend, saying something along the lines of "I can't believe you didn't tell me how tough this course is!" When I think of this I'm a little embarrassed because it is very out of character for me to yell at someone for something like that. I was actually mad at myself, not him. I was out of shape, and how stupid was I to run a 100-miler 10 weeks after having a C-section? Not to mention that I was dead tired since Jackson never let me sleep through the night!

But I had really wanted to do this 100-miler, just to show myself that I could still run that far. I felt that if I went too long without running an ultra, I might not get back into it again. Anyway, that was my "practice run."

The Chicago Marathon was the first week in October. My husband, Jim, was in shape and wanted to do it, so we went together. (My sister, Debbie, came from Wisconsin to watch Jackson.) I needed only a 3:40 time to qualify for Boston, and I intended to pretty much hit that number and be satisfied. As it happened, I was running along with two guys, just keeping it steady, not thinking much about the time. When I finished, I was shocked to see that I had done a 3:18: I qualified with room to spare. And Jim ran an amazing 3:15.

The Boston Marathon is always on a Monday in April. I had made a plane reservation that would allow me to arrive a day early, meet my sister in Boston, and share a hotel room with her the night before the race. Jim had agreed to stay home in Tucson with Jackson and the other two boys, Tim and Andrew. (It was tax season and Jim is an accountant, so it was no small gift for him to assume full child-care duties!) Getting to the race was going to be a little complicated. Southwest Airlines—a sponsor of the Tucson Marathon, of which I'm the director—had given me a free ticket, so I was flying out of their Phoenix "hub" airport. Because Southwest doesn't fly into Boston, I had to fly to Baltimore and then figure out how to get to Boston. Everyone was saying, "Take the train," but I'd never taken a train in my life and didn't even know *how* to take a train. It did seem like the best alternative, so I decided I would just have to figure that out.

And then I heard about the Mule Mountain Marathon.

The Mule Mountain race was in Sierra Vista, Arizona, about 70 miles from Tucson. I had run it before and liked it, but I had not planned to do it this year until I heard that the organizers had put up a $1,000 prize for the first woman to cross the finish line. That's almost unheard of in distance running, where there's not a lot of money floating around. Unless you have a very generous sponsor—which I didn't at the time—all your running expenses are paid out-of-pocket. A thousand dollars would really help—if I could win. So I wanted to go for it.

Unfortunately, Mule Mountain would be run on the Saturday before Boston. The schedule was going to be rather tight. I also foresaw a lot of *extra* running—through airports and railroad stations. But I was sure I could handle it.

My father drove me to Sierra Vista, and he would be driving me straight to the Phoenix airport after the race. I had my bags all packed—carry-on only, because if I were going to catch a train in Baltimore, I wouldn't have time to wait at the airport baggage claim.

The Mule Mountain course began at about 5,000 feet, climbed for a while, passed through a tunnel, continued with a 9-mile downhill, and then ramped up into another climb. The U.S. Army organized the event. They did a good job of it too. Everything had a kind of military precision.

The unusual purse had brought some fast runners to Mule Mountain. I don't think of myself as superfast, but I'm very consistent. I never stop. It's much more dangerous to stop than to slow down. I'll give an example. Have you ever been on a long car trip with a bunch of kids? "Look, there's a McDonald's! Can we stop? Please? Oh, ple-e-eze! We want a Happy Meal! We want a

Happy Meal!" And it goes on like that until you just can't stand to hear the words *Happy Meal* even one more time—so you stop. Strategically, that's a mistake, because for every minute you stop, you're going to have to drive 2 minutes to reach your destination— since you've got to make up not only the time you weren't moving but also the distance you *would have covered* in that time. It's just a mathematical certainty. And if you got tired of hearing *Happy Meal*, wait till you've heard "Are we there yet?" about 12 million times.

In any case, up on Mule Mountain I did my thing. About halfway through the race I was the third woman, but there were some speedsters up ahead of me. Fortunately, there were two of them. As sometimes happens in horse racing, these two got into a duel for the lead. First one, then the other would pull ahead. Luckily for me, they wore each other out. I was able to pass them as they began to droop.

Then something happened that was completely new to me. Some sort of official vehicle appeared right beside me. It was a little distracting, but it was probably supposed to be a sort of honor guard since I was the lead woman. I had asked my father to watch for me at a point near the 20-mile mark of the race to hand me a pack of GU. (There are all different kinds of squeeze-pack energy gels now, but GU was the first and, at the time, the only one.) I wanted to get an extra boost of calories for the last leg of the race. Sure enough, there he was, waiting for me. I'd also asked him to let me know, if he could, where the next closest woman was in the race.

Dad handed me the GU, but then I had a thought. Some of these races have very strict rules about what you can ingest. At some you aren't permitted to eat or drink anything during the race that wasn't officially provided. I wasn't sure what the rules were for this race, and since I was leading, I didn't want to blow it by getting disqualified for some stupid reason. So I didn't eat the GU after all, but I still wanted to know what was going on behind me. I was confident that the two "rabbits" had taken each other out, but I'm always concerned about someone unexpected sneaking up on me, which has happened a couple of times.

It looked like that might be happening again. Dad told me there was another woman only about a quarter of a mile back. Yikes! Now I'd have to really hammer it. No more "steady as she goes." From the point of view of an ultrarunner, marathons can be quite intense. Twenty-six miles seems like a long way to a nonrunner, but when you're used to pacing yourself over 50 or 100 miles, 26 can seem compressed. The good news was that though I thought my dad was at mile 20, where I'd asked him to meet me, he actually was at mile 23! It was like getting 3 free miles.

Well, as the slogan advises, I "just did it." I was the winning woman, and $1,000 richer. My dad had been correct: Another woman had been close behind me, but she was part of a relay group of recreational runners, each of whom was doing a quarter of the race. Even if she had passed me, I still would have been the official winner. For this I had totally knocked myself out. Pretty funny, but there really wasn't any time to sit around and laugh about it. Nor was there time to bask in my very first overall women's win. I had to get started on the next leg of the weekend's events, getting across the country as quickly as possible.

My ever-reliable father drove me 200 miles to the airport in Phoenix, and I was able to get some rest on the plane. As soon as the flight landed, however, I was rushing again to catch a taxi to the railroad station. I had only 25 minutes to catch the train, and when I got to the station, no ticket window was open. All I could think to do was to get on the train anyway, without knowing whether I would be thrown off at the next station. I was relieved to discover that it wasn't a big deal to buy a ticket from the conductor on the train.

Once we were under way, I had another opportunity to relax. It was late at night by this time, so I really needed to sleep. But I was very keyed up. As I've said, this was my first train ride. The train wasn't that full, and as it stopped in Philadelphia and then New York and a few people boarded my car, I felt like they were checking me out. I had no idea if it was safe to leave my bags in the overhead rack while I slept, so I piled them around me, draping my body over them and trying to convince myself I was comfortable.

That was on Saturday night. On Sunday, just as I'd hoped, my sister and I had the whole day to look around Boston. We did the Paul Revere walk together; that was really neat. Then, at noon on Monday, I ran my second marathon in 3 days.

Just a funny side note: For some reason, when I got to the starting line of the Boston, I was starving. In all the excitement I just hadn't thought much about eating. I did have dinner the night before—at least I'm pretty sure I did, but I couldn't remember it. I saw another runner eating a pack of GU and I asked if he had an extra. He did, and I ate it—for real this time.

It was a busy weekend, one that would leave most people breathless, I suspect. But for me it was fun, and it was the kind of stress that, weirdly enough, I find calming. This is something paradoxical about me: I find peace of mind in extreme activity.

[ONE]

WHERE I STARTED

CHAPTER 1

WHY WRITE?
WHY RUN?

I went to college at Michigan Tech, in northern Michigan. Each February the college hosted a winter carnival that featured snow and ice sculptures created by members of the campus's fraternities and sororities. Some of those sculptures were impressive, with an amazing amount of detail—true works of art. There were ice airplanes. There were snow ocean liners. There were Snoopy doghouses. The sculptors must have worked really hard over several weeks.

Houghton, Michigan, is really cold in the winter, and sometimes the sculptures lasted for weeks after the carnival. But then, eventually, they were gone. Maybe the people who worked on them would remember them, and I'm sure pictures were taken, but the sculptures were forgotten by everybody else. It seemed poignant that people would put so much time and effort into something that turned into water and literally went down the drain. But that's exactly what happened: Perfectly good Snoopy doghouses were allowed to simply melt away. It seemed like a waste.

Sometimes I think that what I do now is not so different from building ice sculptures. And I don't want it to just disappear.

I'm an ultrarunner. I run *really* long distances. A marathon, for example, always covers a distance of 26.2 miles. For most people, that's a long way. Technically, anything over that distance is considered an ultra, but the shortest ultra events are at least 50 kilometers, and most races are much longer. Competing takes great physical conditioning and the ability to sustain your concentration, but because it isn't very exciting to watch, ultrarunning gets little attention from the mainstream media. There are very few spectators, and I'd venture to say that many people don't even know the sport exists.

Some in the ultrarunning community are indifferent to this lack of attention, and some actually prefer it. Being under the media's radar seems like a way for the sport to remain pure, free of the drugs and other issues that have affected track stars and pro athletes. If that's the plan, it's working. There are usually about 50 people at the finish line of the Badwater Ultramarathon, a premier ultrarunning event—and about half of those people are the staff and administrators of the event itself. Most of the rest aren't spectators either. The Badwater finish line is also the trailhead for climbing the highest mountain in the lower 48 states, so sometimes a runner struggling through the final yards of the race has to dodge minivans filled with hikers heading into a nearby parking lot.

Yet Badwater is an amazing event. It has been described as one of the toughest races in the world. It covers 135 miles, crossing Death Valley and ascending 8,000 feet up Mount Whitney. The race always takes place in mid- to late July, when the Death Valley heat is usually 120 to 130 degrees. Runners are allowed up to 60 hours to complete the course. But if you want to finish among the leaders, you've got to cover the distance in *well* under a day and a half. That means no sleeping and minimal stopping. The winning time is usually in the range of 25 to 30 hours. In 2002, when I was the overall winner of the race, I set the current women's record of 27:56.

In the desert heat, some people hallucinate. Although I've never seen any mirages, I do think that running Badwater and other ultra events is a unique experience. It's a perspective I'd like to share, which is the reason I've decided to write this book. I want to create a written record of the challenges, changes, and insights that running has brought to me. I feel like I've been to a really unusual country and I want to tell you what that place was like. But I also want to tell how I got to that country, why I decided to travel there, and why I'm always eager to return. It's an exciting place, totally unpredictable and a little dangerous.

Late-night talk-show host and comedian David Letterman, who's a runner himself, is one of the few media personalities who's given attention to ultrarunning. In 2003, when I was the overall winner of Badwater for the second year in a row, David invited me to be a guest on his show. I thought he struck the perfect note of appreciation for what ultrarunners accomplish as well as amusement at what it involves. He asked me what I had won, what the prize was. I told him it was a belt buckle. "A belt buckle?" Reaching for a pad of paper and a pen, David leaned toward me and asked conspiratorially, "How can I get in on this?"

Then David asked me whether I thought women could expect to win against men in these grueling races. I answered that I thought women might actually have an advantage. Maybe, I suggested, we were somehow hardwired to endure more pain. Maybe it had something to do with the fact that it's women who give birth to children. David shot me one of his patented quizzical glances. "But you didn't actually have a child during the race, did you?" he asked. When I laughed and said that no, I had not, he nodded knowingly.

"No, of course not. Because running across Death Valley in July is one thing—but having a child during the race? That would be crazy."

When people first hear about ultrarunning, they often wonder what kind of individual could possibly get involved with it. Their view is the same as David Letterman's: "This is crazy. What kind of person would do something like that?"

I think the answer to that question would have to be "A person just like you in many ways. But also different."

I should say that I have always been a sauna freak—I hate the cold; I just love being hot. When I was in college, I took part in a study of the effects of heat and moisture on the human body. I was placed in a room where the temperature was 100 degrees and the humidity was 100 percent. It was a real hothouse. Then I was given my instructions: "Pam, here's an exercise bicycle that we'd like you to pedal for about an hour. Do you think that will be a problem?"

"Not at all!" I said, and I started my superheated ride to nowhere. An hour later, my core temperature was tested. It had elevated by only 1 degree. The other volunteers experienced much greater changes. I didn't win anything, not even a belt buckle, but I did learn something about my physiology that I'm sure has helped me in some of my races—I'm not that affected by high temperatures. My lack of response to heat is just something I was born with. It's not something that I developed through training, so I can't take credit for it. It's just one way I'm different from other people.

To some extent, what makes me different is a matter of degree. Lots of people like to run. They just don't run as far as I do, or as often. But even among ultrarunners I'm different. Many of them are able to devote almost all their emotional energy to the sport. I have a family—quite a large family—and all the excitement that goes with it. Altogether, there are five children: two I had with Steve, my first husband; one I had with Jim, to whom I've been

6

married for 15 years; and two are Jim's from his previous marriage and live with their mother.

Most people who have been running for a while, even in a very casual way, mentally set a limit on how much they can do. Some people might feel that 10 kilometers (6.2 miles) is a distance they can handle, but don't see themselves going much beyond that. Others might try a half-marathon. Or the limit might be expressed in terms of time rather than distance. Maybe they've done a marathon in 4½ hours but harbor no hope of breaking the 4-hour mark.

Placing limits on what I think I can accomplish is something I tend not to do. I've heard that people are actually able to cover about twice their imagined limit: If you think you can run only 1 mile, you can really run 2; if you think you can run 2, you can run 4. You might not be able to cut your "best" time in half, but you can reduce it by a significant percentage. That has been my experience. While initially I never thought I would run the distances I have, or in the times in which I've done them, I haven't really put mental limitations on myself either. And truly, I've surprised myself.

And now I have some stories to tell.

CHAPTER 2

WHERE I COME FROM

I n many ways, my life has followed a very conventional path. I got
married when I was in my early twenties, had children, divorced,
and remarried. In business, I've been an entrepreneur, serving as
race director of the Tucson Marathon. I certainly don't live the life
of a star professional athlete. I go to the supermarket. I get stuck in
traffic jams. I have days when I really feel up and days when I feel
just the opposite.

I was born in a small town in the Midwest, specifically in the
Upper Peninsula, or UP, of Michigan—an area at the northern
border of the United States that pushes into Lake Superior. It's
pretty there, but the prettiness is hard to appreciate during winters
that are freezing cold and summers that swarm with mosquitoes.
There's a saying about the weather in the UP: It's 11 months of
winter and 1 month of bad sledding.

My hometown, Palmer, Michigan, had a population of about 500.
It consisted of a central section of family homes about 6 blocks long
and 6 blocks wide, surrounded by larger family properties and the

9

Northern Michigan woods. It wasn't a "town" like those with a downtown area of shops and services. It was a two-lane street—one lane of traffic going in each direction—with smaller roads lined with houses running off to one side. Spaced about a quarter-mile apart were a gas station, a post office, and a grocery story. On the other side of the road, off in the distance, was an iron mine.

What I liked about Palmer were the large front and backyards that virtually all the homes had. Physical activity was my preoccupation from a very early age. Though I was a solid student academically, I thought of school mainly as a place where I could challenge other kids to contests and races of all kinds—and by *other kids*, I mean boys. The girls were never serious enough about sports as far as I was concerned. Boys were more competitive, but right from the start they gave me the feeling that I was bugging them when I wanted to compete in some race or game.

I enjoyed a few other activities that didn't involve racing, at least initially. My mother taught me to swim, and that sport became a lifelong love. She also spent countless hours driving me and my only sibling, Debbie, back and forth to ballet lessons—something I was not particularly suited to. The slow, controlled movements of ballet tested my last young nerve until my mom had the better idea to move me into tap dancing. That was more my speed. And speaking of speed, I also had a cool yellow minibike that I'd begged my parents for. I was surprised when they gave in and got me one, but I loved every minute of speeding down the back alleys of Palmer and into the woods around town.

My mother, Karen Saari, was a hardworking woman who balanced her entrepreneurial career with life in a community where most wives stayed home. Her family comes from Chicago, so it must have required an adjustment for her when she landed in a backwater like the UP. After getting her nursing degree, she worked in a hospital as an RN and later became director of nursing. After that, she worked in a nursing home that she and a partner eventually purchased before building two others. Like other businesswomen of her generation, she was breaking new ground; most of those at the top of her industry were men. I don't think she got much support from colleagues. Still, she was able to accomplish a lot.

Mom definitely instilled the values of initiative and assertiveness in her two daughters. She completed everything she started. And she saw to it that my older sister and I were the same way. She enjoyed outdoor sports like snowmobiling and cross-country skiing despite suffering from back pain for as long as I can remember. She was used to pain, and she didn't overvalue it. I'm sure seeing that quality in her had an effect on me. Sheer willpower allowed her to live a purposeful and productive life. Watching her, I learned a lot about what someone can accomplish with hard work. I also learned why leaving the Upper Peninsula would be a good idea.

There was a family legend about my grandfather—my mom's dad—that might provide a clue to my predisposition for going extreme distances. He was a guy who liked to argue. It didn't matter what the topic was. If you said today is Thursday, he would say that it is Wednesday. He was a really caring person—he'd give you the shirt off his back if you needed it—but he just had this contrary way about him. He also was a very hard worker. My mother remembers that for 18 years, from the time he was in his late forties until he retired at 65, he worked two full-time jobs. He worked in the railroad yard during the day—which was very cold during the Chicago winters—and at night he was a ticket taker for the transit system.

The family lore that I mentioned was set in the early 1930s, so Grandfather would have been—I'm just guessing—in his fifties. Mom's family was having a get-together in Merrill, Wisconsin, about 300 miles north of Chicago. My grandfather got into an argument about something and stalked out of the house. In itself, this was not unusual. But this time, he kept on going. He actually walked all the way back home to Chicago! When he arrived there, the story goes, the soles of his shoes were completely gone.

My father, Roy Saari, was also a very determined person. When I was a girl, he worked at the iron mine across the road, said to be the largest open-pit mine in the world. He used to wake up at 3:30 in the morning, have some coffee, and then leave for the mine within the hour. When he returned in mid-afternoon, the second part of his day began, which could include everything from building an addition onto our house to making sure the car had a full tank of gas. My father naturally took responsibility for tasks of all kinds. Looking back, I can see how much I came to take this for granted. Once, when I was a teenager, I got a flat tire out on the highway. Several people stopped to offer help, but I told them there was no need to go to any trouble: "I'll just call my dad!"

Though I didn't see this side of him while I was growing up, I knew that my dad had been competitive. He'd been a ski jumper when he was a teenager. Unfortunately, he'd taken a bad fall when he was 16, and that was pretty much the end of that.

So the seeds of my running career must have been planted in my childhood, but at the time I had no idea that seeds were being planted for anything. I was just very energetic and very competitive, and I never liked to slow down. For me, happiness meant being outdoors in open space.

Many, many days were spent at our family's cabin in Beaver Lake, in northern Wisconsin, a 4-hour drive from our home in Palmer. Visits might last a week or a weekend, depending on how long Mom and Dad could stay away from their jobs. Even though I did love playing outside, I can't say that going to the cabin was my favorite thing. There was no running water, no electricity, and no toilet. The outhouse was situated way too far from the cabin, in my opinion. It seemed like it was at least a quarter of a mile away, which was far from convenient if you had to go at night. Mice made their homes in the outhouse, so before entering I would always kick at the door and yell, "Get out of the way, I'm coming in." Once, after leaving the outhouse, I encountered a huge porcupine on the path back to the house. It was as big as a small bear. I screamed for my father, who came running with a shovel since his rifles had been stolen by vandals a while before. Porcupines will eat your house and they do have those quills, so both for practical purposes and because I was terrified, my dad smacked the porcupine to death right in front of me. The quills flew all over the place.

My better memories of Beaver Lake are a blur of swimming and running. If a game involved chasing someone or being chased, I was in it. Occasionally, there were quieter pursuits—berry picking or fishing with my dad. I honestly didn't care very much about fishing, but I did like spending time with my father.

We spent quite a lot of time at the lake in the winter, too. We took along snowmobiles for countless hours of riding and exploring. We'd drive into the deepest backwoods and dart between the hardwood trees. The snowmobiles were also necessary to transport us from the main road to our cabin, because the driveways and side roads were completely snowed in. I am no fan of the cold, but I was fine as long as I was sufficiently bundled up or riding in front of my father, leaning back into his relative warmth.

Skiing was a favorite pastime for most of my family; Debbie was a good skier, but not me. I really hated it. I was never warm enough, so whenever hitting the slopes was the family plan for the day, I'd balk, whining and complaining that I didn't want to go. Once, when I was 5, I broke my leg skiing at Ishpeming, Michigan. I've often thought that I might have done it subconsciously just to prove my point about how awful skiing was. The snow there was powdery, not the hard-packed snow we were used to. I was going down the hill when one leg went one way and the other went the other, and down I went. It wasn't a very serious break—just enough to prove my point. But it still hurt plenty on the way to the hospital.

Through it all, there was an atmosphere of self-reliance and pioneer spirit that usually was fun but could lead to some intense moments. One time when I was 10 or 11 years old, my dad was outside chopping wood. Nothing unusual there! Suddenly, he appeared on the porch of the house with a blood-soaked rag pressed to his forehead. Somehow the double-bladed ax he was using had slipped, giving him a mean cut. I was really shocked. I'm not sure if I was crying, as my sister was, but I was very frightened.

As a nurse, Mom knew that Dad needed treatment beyond what she could provide at the cabin, so without any further conversation we got on the snowmobiles and headed for the nearest hospital— which was not exactly just around the corner. As soon as Dad's forehead was stitched up, we got back on the snowmobiles and returned to the cabin, where Dad went back to chopping wood.

Physical toughness was a strong point in my family, and maybe in the Upper Peninsula as a whole. It was cultivated and bred into us over many generations, so it came easily to us. It was expected of us, and it was what we expected of ourselves.

There were a lot of people like us in the UP. If it was 5:00 in the morning and the lights weren't on in somebody's house, people would say to them, "So you slept in this morning, eh?" It was said jokingly, but the message was that everybody was supposed to be up and at 'em before sunrise. If somebody died, no one said, "He was a nice guy," or "She had a great sense of humor." They said, "He knew how to work," or "She was a real good worker." It didn't matter whether it was a man or a woman. The Upper Peninsula may not have encouraged entrepreneurship or higher achievement in women, but it definitely encouraged work.

That was how things were done when I was growing up. The core values were self-sufficiency, stamina, and hard work—traits that I've tried to put to use during my running career.

CHAPTER 3

I WAS OLGA KORBUT

As I've said, I had always been into games and sports. These consisted mostly of improvised races, dance classes, and generally bouncing off the walls. I had been introduced to gymnastics in phys ed at school, and already I was among the best in my class. So, though I had never been much of a TV watcher, I, like millions of other Americans, was glued to the couch during the 1972 Olympics, watching 17-year-old Soviet gymnast Olga Korbut prance along the balance beam.

Olga's historic moment, so to speak, was fraught with drama. Everyone seemed to be captivated by the triumphs and tragedies of her performances. She was not even a full-fledged member of the Soviet team—she was only at the Olympics as an alternate because another athlete had been injured. She was a dark horse, and I very much identified with that.

Even though Olga was a media sensation from the first moment she appeared, her scores were not impressive at the outset. She gave an especially poor performance on the uneven bars. Out of a possible 10 points, she was only in the mid-7s—really bad scores for an Olympic athlete. The image of Olga weeping with her head in her hands was broadcast around the world, and it stirred the sympathy of millions.

The following night, Olga came back stronger than ever. She won gold medals for balance beam and floor exercise, and a silver medal on the uneven bars. Her backflip on the beam was one of the most electrifying moments in Olympic history.

As an impressionable kid with a passion for gymnastics, I was beyond smitten—I was obsessed. From that moment, I lived and breathed the sport. I practiced gymnastics every minute that I could, in the basement, off the couch, wherever I happened to be. I bugged my parents steadily enough that they bought me a regulation tumbling mat for our basement. I spent long hours down there doing flips and somersaults.

Gymnastics in general, and Olga in particular, were the perfect physical expressions of what had been going on in my head for quite a while. There were lots of things about Olga that I related to. She was from the outback of the Soviet Union, just as I was from a remote part of the United States. She was small and quick, just like me. Also, she was obviously very dedicated to her sport. At 4 feet 11 and 84 pounds, she looked like a pixie. But once an event started, she radiated concentration and performed powerfully. Then, as soon as it was over, she was all smiles, a real crowd pleaser.

Lots of girls got caught up in the Olga craze that year, wearing their hair in two little pigtails like her and practicing cartwheels and flips. To me, Olga Korbut was completely inspiring. I could imagine myself, through lots of hard work, being like her: an accomplished and polished world-class gymnast. It was a dream that perfectly matched the potential that I already was showing, and I was beginning to see how becoming really good at something might be my ticket to the larger world outside of Palmer, Michigan.

I practiced and exercised quite intensely every day, and I knew I needed to keep it up. I was small, and at 14, I started noticing that my friends were beginning to fill out, to develop hips and breasts. To look like them was the last thing I wanted. To be competitive—which in my mind meant being as good as Olga Korbut—I had to *look* like Olga Korbut: small, wiry, flat as a board. While most girls my age were looking forward to maturing physically, I was determined not to go there. I made a conscious decision to stop eating.

In my mind, this wasn't about low self-esteem or a desire to disappear or any of the other pressures that are usually associated with anorexia. I can't say that I was influenced by so-called cultural images of skinny models and actresses. I had never identified with that facet of popular culture, so I didn't care at all about looking good in that sense. My motivation was to be competitive at the top level, to make whatever sacrifices might be necessary to be the best. I've thought about this quite a lot over the years, and I think such an impulse is more common than many people realize. With gymnastics, as with dance, a particular aesthetic, a certain look, is expected. You hear about ballet dancers who don't get to perform because they're too "heavy." They're perfectly capable of dancing, but they don't look right. Or, rather, they don't look the way people expect a ballet dancer to look. Weight is an issue even in sports where it's not about a "look." If a ski jumper is tall, he or she uses longer skis, which is an advantage. Tall and skinny ski jumpers are lighter and have an even bigger advantage.

My determination to do well in sports spurred my determination to not let my body change. This proved to be a potent and sometimes dangerous combination that operated in my life for a long time. The stoic persistence that helped me to work so hard in gymnastics was put to work in a new direction: starving myself. I very nearly stopped eating completely. I would not drink milk or ingest anything that would put weight on my body. This obsession really took hold of me. It was in full force for the next 15 years, and I wouldn't be honest if I said that it's completely gone now.

If my parents were aware of the drama that was going on in my head, they didn't have time to dwell on it. They were both working hard. No one acted as if my love for gymnastics or my nonstop physical activity was particularly unusual or any cause for concern. It was just "my thing."

It's interesting how the same event can mean very different things to different people—and to some people, nothing at all. For a fan of a college or pro football team, a weekend game may be the most important thing in the world. Other people aren't even aware that the game is taking place, or may see it but soon forget about it. In the same way, lots of people were really excited by the '72 Olympics and the terrific little gymnast who was the bright counterpoint to the devastating kidnapping and murder of the Israeli athletes. But long after most people had moved on in their lives, Olga Korbut for me was still a lightning rod for some of my most important feelings.

Four years later, when I watched the next Olympics, I had a different, though still strong, reaction. While I didn't understand this at the time, I can see now that before the games started the world was waiting to see who would be the next Olga Korbut, the next one the media could fall in love with.

The next one, of course, was Nadia Comaneci, the Romanian gymnast who turned out to be an even bigger worldwide sensation than Olga. You'd think I would have been just as excited about Nadia as I had been about Olga—after all, Nadia was also 4 feet 11 and 86 pounds. Surprisingly, I just couldn't appreciate her in the same way. Instead of focusing on what Nadia actually did in her events, I was outraged by the fact that she was awarded a perfect score by the judges. Especially since she didn't get just one 10—she got seven of them! That wasn't right. No one could be that perfect.

I think it's possible that I also was offended by the apparent ease of her accomplishments. Unlike Olga, who obviously had had to work hard for her achievements, success almost seemed to have been handed to Nadia. That was not the way things were done where I came from! The idea of what in my mind was unearned success just didn't sit well.

Maybe I was also affected by the way Olga Korbut had become old news by this time. Although she again competed for the Soviet Union in 1976, she didn't get much attention. In fact, she wasn't even the best gymnast on the Russian team. Out with the old, in with the new.

I honestly don't remember exactly what my feelings were at that time. I only know that for better *and* for worse, I was completely awed by Olga. In a way, I wanted to *be* Olga. Even today, I often think of her with deep admiration.

CHAPTER 4

MY BRAIN, PART ONE:
A UNIQUE DISORDER

I'm sure that all people are, to some extent, mysteries to themselves. There are things about myself that I still don't understand, despite my having invested a lot of time, effort, and pain in trying to figure them out. My anorexia is probably the most glaring example of this. Over the years I've looked at it from many angles with the help of many people, and still there are questions about it that haven't been answered.

I've said that identifying with Olga Korbut was the trigger for anorexia in my life. Of course, I didn't understand that for a very long time. When I saw Olga in the Olympics, I just saw what I wanted to be. When I looked around at girls my age and a little older, I saw what I didn't want to be. I wanted to be thin and athletic; allowing my body to develop would have made me the opposite of that. It became a game. The object was to eat as little as possible, and the prize was the body of an Olympic gymnast.

That is how I remember it. But I really can't be sure whether my interest in Olga was the cause of my eating issue or just the trigger for a tendency that was already in place. I wish I could be more definite about this. No one, however, not even cutting-edge researchers, seems certain of when, how, or why anorexia develops in an individual human being.

Is it the result of a certain kind of upbringing or environment? It is true that meals in our house were often a time for arguments. Voices were raised, sometimes about whether I was eating enough, but often about whatever problem seemed most important at the time. Maybe this created an association in my mind between eating and anxiety. That has been suggested by the psychiatrists and therapists I've seen over the years. But looking to anyone else's actions for the cause of my anorexia does not sit comfortably with me. I don't blame anyone—certainly not my mother or father—for anything. Mom and Dad didn't prevent me from eating. Neither did anybody or anything else in Palmer, Michigan.

Anorexia may originate at a level deeper than the dinner table or the hometown. Perhaps it's somehow hardwired into the genetic code. I'm a little skeptical of this, however, because whenever something seems beyond our understanding, the fallback explanation seems to be DNA. I'm not saying that's wrong, I'm just saying that it seems like a convenient way out.

I've made a lot of progress, but anorexia is an ongoing experience for me. It's an issue that loomed very large in my past, that is not nearly as large now, and that I hope will become even less of a presence as time goes on. In addition to having had formal treatment, I've read a lot about anorexia over the years. I've also spoken with many other people who are dealing with this problem. This started when my mother first took me to a doctor, and it continues to this day.

Here are a few of the things I've learned: At some point in life, between 1.5 million and 7 million American women (about 0.5 to 3.5 percent) will have some form of this disease (not including other eating disorders, like bulimia). It will also affect a number of boys, but significantly fewer. It mostly affects young women, though in some people, the disease doesn't manifest until later in life. For one in five of those who have this problem, it will be deadly.

The disease (or disorder) can take so many different forms in its specifics that it seems almost to tailor itself to the individual. Maybe because of this, there is a blanket diagnostic category called EDNOS, or Eating Disorder Not Otherwise Specified.

I recently learned of a newly defined subcategory of anorexia that seems on its face to be directly applicable to me. This is *anorexia athletica*, a syndrome specifically tagged to eating issues associated with athletics.

In a way, it's really exciting to hear about this: "Look, a diagnosis just for Pam!" But upon further investigation, I've run into some of the same reservations that I have about other theories of anorexia. I'm not saying that any of this is wrong. I'm just saying that it doesn't completely apply to me. Still, looking closely at the concept of anorexia athletica gives me an opportunity to share my experiences with an eating disorder. I'll also be able to show why I think my experiences may be both similar to those of other people and also different in some very important ways.

Someone with anorexia athletica is defined by eight criteria:

1. Repeated exercising beyond the requirements for good health. By standard measures, I'm sure I would fall into this category. But what constitutes good health for one individual might not be good enough for another. Running for 3 hours every day might put some people in the hospital. I am certain that *not* running for 3 hours every day would very quickly make me ill. The other thing I need to say is that when you are an elite athlete, it really can't be considered *exercise* any more. You could say that exercise is my *job*.

2. Fanatical attention to weight and diet. Inarguably, over the
years I have been fanatical about my weight as well as the shape of
my body. However, I don't think I was ever fanatical about my diet.
I've never really made a big emotional investment in food. Still, the
longer I compete, the more I have to think about my diet. I'll say
more about this later.

3. Stealing exercise time from work and relationships. I am
inclined to plead guilty to this, but I'm uncomfortable with the
word *stealing*. There's a sneaky aspect to stealing that has never been
part of my running. I'm really up-front about it and I always have
been. There are times when I feel guilty about the hours I devote to
my sport, but if I don't devote those hours I feel guilty too. The
guilt is limited to my relationships with my family; I don't feel bad
about taking time from my work, because the Tucson Marathon
doesn't require year-round, 9-to-5 attention. In the fall, as the
marathon approaches, I give it whatever amount of time is needed,
whether it cuts into my running or not. It's amazing how trying to
meet the expectations of 4,000 runners can make you focus!

4. Focusing on the challenge, and forgetting that exercise can be
fun. At the elite level of racing, the challenge is what it's all about.
For a serious runner, emphasizing fun seems to devalue the concept
of running. Forgive me if this sounds arrogant, but would we say
that painters or musicians who work hard at perfecting their art
should think more about having fun with it? When I'm running
throughout the day, I'm not concerned about the challenge. I run
with our dog and with friends at whatever speed they want to go,
and I have fun. That said, the challenge *is* fun, too!

5. Defining self-worth in terms of performance. Not guilty again.
Whether it's in running or anything else, I'm able to separate what
I am from what I do. I think of myself as an extremely consistent
person, as an athlete and as a personality. Pam is still Pam whether
she wins a race or comes in last or doesn't finish. I've been doing this

a long time. I don't think I can really surprise myself. When I was the overall winner of Badwater 2 years in a row, I didn't start thinking of myself as the greatest athlete in the world. And when I dropped out of the Leadville Trail 100 in 2005, I didn't imagine that I had discovered some deep, dark truth about my self-worth.

6. Being rarely or never satisfied with athletic achievements. I am occasionally disappointed by my performance on a given day, but overall I am proud of my achievements. I have good days and bad days, and I never waste time kicking myself about something that happened yesterday or the day before. What I do at a specific moment in an event is always exactly what I want to do at that moment. Nobody ever twists my arm. Since I take total responsibility for my actions, how can I not be satisfied with them? I never replay the race in my mind, especially if it involves beating myself up about something. The closest I come to dissatisfaction might be to plan on doing something differently tomorrow, based on what I learned today. I want that to be a forward-looking attitude, not a self-punishing one.

7. Not savoring victory. Pushing on to the next challenge immediately. Right! Not only do I fail to "savor" victory, I don't even really believe in it. I rarely think about beating other runners. I think about doing my best in the race I'm in and then doing my best in the next one. In a way, it's all one big race to me, so victory is not really an operative concept. And speaking of savoring victory, I rarely attend the dinners or parties that are often held after races. It's not that I'm a party pooper. After a long race, my first thought is to regroup with my family. And then I really and truly do want to "push on to the next challenge immediately." Yes, this is actually what I desire. There may be people who think that I'm doing this because of some compulsion or as a way to compensate for something. To me, the desire for the next race is absolutely authentic. As someone once said, "Cockfighting may be wrong.

But what the hell else does a fighting cock want to do?"

8. Justifying excessive behavior by defining self as an elite athlete. But I *am* an elite athlete. It actually took me a long time to really recognize that. Truthfully, it was a lot easier to see myself as someone who just liked to get out there and run. I struggle with the term *elite* but have to acknowledge it does apply to me. And as an elite athlete, I now feel a real responsibility to compete in major events. This takes discipline and commitment; self-justification is not part of it. There have been times when I have tried to justify *not* taking part in a race. I've usually been able to resist that impulse. Now that I'm trying to take myself seriously as a runner, I don't expect to have many problems of that kind in the future. I am more excited and committed to ultrarunning than ever. I would never say that I'm an elite swimmer or an elite gymnast, but I am an elite runner. I'm a two-time national champion in the 24-hour run, a two-time overall winner of the Badwater Ultramarathon, and the national women's age-group (40 to 44) record holder in the 48-hour run. I want to live up to that reality. That is so important to me. It definitely is something much larger than a rationale for anorexic behavior.

• • • • •

One of the things that bothers me about these criteria—and in fact about all the therapies I've had for anorexia—is the implication that the "normal" person is someone who's not too excited about, much less totally committed to, anything. I know some people may want to argue with me about this, but to me, what passes for "normalcy" seems to be the absence of real devotion, not to mention passion. Where would that leave the people who have been the greats in any field? When you have a gift, there is often a dark side. That just seems to be the way things work. One of the biggest challenges of my life has been making sure that the dark side doesn't win.

CHAPTER 5

HIGH SCHOOL

I cannot say that upon entering Negaunee High School I experienced any increased interest in academics. My friends were mostly the brighter students and my grades were always acceptable, but that just wasn't where my heart lay. I was pretty popular in school. My nickname was Motormouth, which is not surprising to anyone who knows me now. Some things haven't changed very much.

I was still into gymnastics, although I'd become more realistic about it. I was no longer trying to be an Olympic champion like Olga Korbut. I'd started playing tennis, and I was on the track team too. Our track coach would lumber out to the field and say, "You've got to run 3 miles," and I'd think, "You're crazy!" Three miles seemed like a long distance to me then, and I hated that kind of running. It was boring to me. So I'd basically cheat, leading my teammates across neighborhood backyards to cut the distance.

In any case, Debbie was the track star of the family. She held the record for the 100-yard dash at our high school for 3 years.

I, meanwhile, quit the track team in my senior year, when I was prevented from doing the relay race that I felt I'd worked hard to be included in. I'd shown up for practice every night, and it seemed to me that girls who were showing up only 2 nights a week were getting plum spots on the relay team. I just didn't feel like knocking myself out anymore.

For all 4 years of high school, I was a cheerleader. I was even the captain of the squad for a couple of years. In the lives of many girls, there's a certain period when they want to be a cheerleader more than anything else in the world. It's a big deal to stand up in front of the student body and fans—you get to be the center of attention in a way, even though the real action is on the field or court. I don't think I was obsessive about it, but cheerleading was really important to me. It was another athletic event—gymnastics with a different uniform, another way to challenge myself. Some girls saw it as dance or an opportunity to flirt with the players. I didn't see it that way. So I had to put up with the rest of the cheerleaders, and they had to put up with me.

One thing that was a little disappointing about cheerleading was the quality of our Negaunee Miners uniforms. While the football team got new uniforms every year, the cheerleaders wore hand-me-downs. The maize-and-blue wool uniforms would be inherited from older cheerleaders as we moved from grade to grade. Freshmen inherited the junior varsity uniforms and then the JVs moved up and had to wear the old varsity uniforms. There must have been 50 boys on the football team, counting the benchwarmers, all with brand-new jerseys. You'd think the school could have come up with a little extra money for new uniforms for seven or eight cheerleaders. Obviously, some priorities at Negaunee were unbalanced. I knew one thing already: I planned to leave the Upper Peninsula.

That plan had more than a little to do with my attraction to Steve Koski, my high school boyfriend, whom I began dating when I was 15. Steve was a year ahead of me in school. His dad was a professional, an engineer, while most Palmer families were blue-collar. Steve was around our house a lot, having dinner with us pretty often and helping my dad with yard work. A few times he even went on trips with us. At first, he was almost like a brother. I'm not sure at what point it turned into something else. I was always aware that Steve was very smart—intelligence is something that has always attracted me—and I could tell that he was not stuck in the rut of doing things the way everybody else did. He dressed with more style and looked less "small town" than the other kids. He reminded me of the way people in Chicago looked. I had a sense that Steve was going to make it out into the larger world beyond the UP, just as I wanted to do. In any case, we seemed to go well together.

I've never thought of myself as a romantic person. Except for the notion that we might get out of town together, I didn't dream up fantasies around Steve. I didn't write love notes or poems to him. The two of us being a couple just seemed normal. When it was time for our senior prom, I did have a nice dress and everything. Unfortunately, just before the prom, Steve got himself into a bit of trouble that derailed what lots of teens think of as the Big Night.

The day of the prom, Steve decided to skip school and go fishing at a nearby lake with a few of his friends. It was just his luck that he was seized with acute appendicitis and had to hitchhike back to town, in a lot of pain, to go to the hospital, where I spent a not-very-romantic evening with him. He probably should have known at that point not to hook up with me—I couldn't help but laugh at him for getting caught playing hooky.

I know most kids think of the prom as a big deal. I didn't really care about missing it.

· · · · ·

At the age of 15, I weighed about 105 pounds. I was doing at least 1,000 situps every day (the minimum I'd permit myself to get away with). I was no longer doing them because I wanted to be in the

Olympics. Working out had sort of taken on a life of its own. But even though it sounds fanatical, it isn't like I didn't know what I was doing. I just liked to be different from everybody else—whatever someone else was doing, I liked to be better at it or do more of it. It's kind of crazy, but it was fun, too.

I'm not sure whether things have changed in the Upper Peninsula, but where I live now, if a child behaved toward food the way I did, there would be a big-time intervention right away. I had pretty much stopped eating. Karen Carpenter's ultimately fatal anorexia hadn't come to light yet, so it's not like the eating disorder was any kind of buzzword or concern. Thirty years ago in Michigan, we really weren't oriented toward seeing problems in each other, especially psychological or emotional problems. It wasn't exactly an introspective environment.

Still, everyone knows that it's not normal to not eat. I can't remember when exactly it became clear to me that I had a problem. It wasn't right away. Eventually, though, I did realize that I was sick.

There are girls for whom anorexia becomes a life-threatening crisis, and you can see that as soon as you look at them. I was never like that. I'm small-boned, so I normally don't carry much weight anyway. Even at around 100 pounds or slightly less, I looked fit and healthy. So, except for a few times when my weight loss seemed to be getting out of hand, I was able to make not eating and compulsive exercising my normal lifestyle without arousing a great deal of concern.

I think I subconsciously determined just how far I could take my "eating issue" before it started to attract attention. It was a bit like playing a game of chicken, which some alcoholics and drug addicts also play. If my parents did see that I had a problem, they weren't inclined to focus on it unless it really got out of control. There were a lot of other things absorbing their attention, mostly related to their work.

When my weight had dropped to 95 pounds, my mom did become really worried and took me to a doctor. This was the first of the many doctors I've seen over the years for anorexia. Some have been much better than others, but this first one definitely was not among the best. Part of the problem was the fact that she was quite overweight. So here was a fat woman trying to tell me that I should be eating more. Needless to say, I didn't find her very convincing. Like a typical teen, I was thinking, "Right. So I'll look like *you?*" She also told me that her daughter was so obese that they had had to install a lock on their refrigerator. Looking back on it, I wonder if this might have been some sort of experimental "laughter therapy." In any case, it didn't work. I still had a long way to go.

I continued playing tennis, practicing with my characteristic ferocity. In my sophomore year of high school, I was the number-two singles player and on the number-one doubles team. Bear in mind that this was all relative. Our coach was just someone who had played some tennis in college. Like a lot of small, rural schools, when it came to hiring coaches, the administration had to scrounge around for anyone who could cover a sport. Locally, there was a golf course, but there were no tennis courts, and I never had a lesson from a pro. When it came time to go to college, I applied to Michigan Tech so I could keep playing tennis. Tech was a Division III school and, frankly, I didn't think I was good enough to compete in a tougher division. I picked Tech mainly because Steve was going there. He'd gotten a full scholarship to study metallurgical engineering. I'd hoped to get an athletic scholarship, but by the time I applied, they had been given out. I was awarded a small sum, about one-tenth of what the scholarships were worth. Ironically, the two women who had gotten the scholarships before I applied did not even make the team.

For many subjects, Michigan Tech is a really good college, but I probably would have gone to whatever school Steve chose. For me, college wasn't about getting a degree from a prestigious university. It was about staying close to a person who was going to go beyond Michigan's borders, and maybe even Wisconsin's borders too. Why, I thought he might even get as far as Chicago.

CHAPTER 6

FROM MICHIGAN
TO TUCSON
TO MICHIGAN
TO TUCSON TO WHERE?

B oth marathons and long trail-running events can take place on two different kinds of courses. On a point-to-point course, runners finish very far from where they started, sometimes by as much as 100 miles. A loop course takes the runners a particular distance and then brings them back to where they began. The psychology of the two types of courses seems to be different. Some runners definitely prefer one kind over the other.

There's also a third option, the one used most often in timed events, like 24-hour runs. It's just doing laps on a running track, often at a high school or public park.

Until recently, making comparisons between my running and

33

my life wasn't something that I did very often. As I get older, though, and reflect on the hundreds of races I've done, I can see that different people choose different routes for themselves. Growing up, I definitely wanted a point-to-point life. The UP was the point where I'd started, and I wanted to go to a point far away and then stay far away. The one thing I didn't want was what I often saw in Palmer: people on a circular track, doing the same things with the same crowd in the same place, and then having kids and setting the kids on the same track. I could never have been satisfied with that.

As I've said, Michigan Tech was in Houghton—a town that was even farther out in the sticks than Palmer. It was funny to me that no one seemed to be aware of this remoteness. Kids at Negaunee would ask me about Houghton, "Do they even have running water there?"

Weirdly enough, even though Steve was a big reason I went to Tech in the first place, I broke up with him during my freshman year to date a guy on the tennis team. He was a good-looking, hard-bodied type—very dramatic. He thought he was Björn Borg. To me, this was exciting. It seems like there are two kinds of guys: the really nice, steady ones and the ones who are not so nice all the time, but rather more of a challenge. My dad and Steve were in the first category. This guy was in the second. It's not that I don't like to be treated well. I guess I'm just susceptible to the attractions of "bad" boys. I like a little more conflict; it's more interesting. This relationship didn't last that long, though, and Steve and I got back together.

When it came to the tennis team, the other female athletes disappointed me. They weren't serious enough! The other women seemed to take the sport lightly. They didn't want to play if they had a test coming up and, given their druthers, they would rather go to a football game than to tennis practice. I wasn't the best player on the team, but I had a very deep athletic work ethic. In the division rankings, I think I was in the low single digits—somewhere around third or fifth—in singles competition and third in doubles, and I worked hard to be there.

At the end of the first year, the coach told us that to make the team the following year we would have to be able to jump rope for 15 minutes straight. My teammates certainly didn't take that seriously. I, however, worked at it all summer. It's really hard to do! Eventually, I was able to do it. The coach had been serious—the girls who barely even tried were cut from the team.

In spite of my unhappiness with my teammates, this was a very good challenge for me. I know that conditioning myself to jump rope for 15 minutes without stopping has really helped me with my breathing even to this day. It gave me an amazingly solid base.

I was majoring in business and was pretty much a B or C student. At Tech, the jocks and the business majors tended to hang out together. Hockey was big at the school, and I liked joking around with the players, challenging them to competitions like doing the most situps or making them jump rope like I'd had to for tennis. It was all in good fun, and we all got better together. I began to teach aerobics, and I ran quite a bit to stay in shape for tennis. At one point, the town of Houghton put on a 10-mile race and some of the hockey players challenged me. I was positive that I'd win, but they *killed* me!

Based on my experiences with the women on the tennis team versus those with the guys on the hockey team, I was beginning to feel that other women didn't share my predilection for going the extra mile. Even for me, as fun as working out or practicing could be, there were more times when it was simply hard work. I think one of the things my parents had instilled in me was the ability to be comfortable with delayed gratification and, really, a willingness to work very hard at something, as if it's a job—you're not always *supposed* to like it, but you still have to do it.

• • • • •

It wasn't much of a surprise when Steve graduated on time, but I didn't. Tech was not a business school per se, and outside its specialties, the academic bar was pretty low. I got an A in English without even being any good or trying. So, after playing a second season of tennis, I transferred to Northern Michigan University in Marquette.

I can't remember exactly when it happened, but Steve and I decided to get married. There was no formal proposal that I can recall. The decision just seemed to happen naturally; it was almost taken for granted by both of us. Steve was already almost part of the family, and now we were going to make it official.

Even if I wasn't exactly swept off my feet, I was somewhat excited about our impending marriage. Mom and I had discussions about my dress. At first I felt that I didn't need a fancy dress or that I could just wear my sister's. Debbie was more into traditional female matters, such as wedding dresses, than I was, and I trusted her judgment. When we were little, Debbie used to go to a lot of trouble dressing her Barbie dolls. Then I'd come along and mess them all up. Now I trusted her fashion sense more than my own. If a dress was good enough for her, it would be good enough for me.

Once I'd decided that, though, I learned from a girl in my dorm that a store in a little town downstate had some really nice wedding dresses. I immediately imagined the town, the store, and the exact dress I wanted—and when we drove down there, there was a dress that was just like the one I'd pictured! I bought it, and just as we were getting back into the car, somebody drove by and sheared the driver's side door right off. There was no way to put it back on. All we could do was to put long strips of duct tape all across the opening to keep my friend from falling out of the car during the drive back to her house.

In retrospect, that probably was not the best omen for the marriage. Not that I noticed it at the time.

The wedding was at our house that my dad had built outside of Gwinn, Michigan. The house was really nice—it was set beside a lake, with lots of sidewalks curving around the exterior. My father loved to lay out sidewalks and was really good at it. These were great for having all sorts of processions at the wedding. The ceremony itself took place beside the lake, under a little trellis. Though it was July, the weather was unseasonably cold. Except for that, the wedding was really nice.

For our honeymoon, my parents treated Steve and me to a Caribbean cruise. When we got the first look at our cabin, I was surprised to discover that our honeymoon lodgings had bunk beds! It was just like being in summer camp. I wanted to ask the steward if we could move to a room with one bed, but Steve wouldn't let me say anything. He preferred to sleep in bunk beds on his honeymoon than to make any waves—another not-so-good omen.

Although I enjoy traveling, I remember surprisingly little about the trip itself. It was actually good to get back to Michigan, especially because I knew we'd soon be leaving again.

Upon graduating, Steve had had 10 or so job offers from companies in all different parts of the country. One was with Duvall, a mining company in Arizona. I didn't know a thing about Arizona except that I'd never been there. So naturally my advice during his deliberations was "Take Arizona!" And that's where we went.

As we departed Michigan, it seemed as though my life was shaping up as a point-to-point event, which was just what I wanted. Soon the UP was thousands of miles behind us.

Since I had not yet gotten my degree, I enrolled at the University of Arizona in Tucson. Steve worked at his job. Tucson was really nice in many ways. Although Arizona is a quite conservative state, Tucson has a different identity. The presence of the university, for instance, gives the city a whole different vibe than you'll find in Phoenix. Tucson is a lot less corporate. The unofficial symbol of the city is the javelina, a funny animal that looks like a wild pig crossed with a German shepherd. It's a city that has a sense of humor about itself.

We had been there for only about a year when Steve announced that he could get a scholarship to earn his master's degree back at Michigan Tech. He wanted to go back to Michigan.

"*What?!*" I thought. We had just *left* Michigan. Steve portrayed this as a smart business move. With an advanced degree, he declared, he would be able to earn more money. There wasn't a lot of discussion. His attitude was "I have spoken." Yet I can't say the move was shoved down my throat, because I don't think I protested very much. Maybe I was homesick. Maybe I was just confused. As my course looped back to Michigan, I'm sure I was a little disturbed. But abandoning course never really occurred to me.

Soon we were back in Houghton, and both of us were again enrolled at Michigan Tech. At least I could play on the tennis team again—that was a plus. We had intended to live in a trailer owned by Steve's father, but when we got there, we discovered that it had been rented out. My mom came to our rescue. When she saw how disappointed I was about the snarl in our plans, she bought a trailer for us. We lived there for a year and a half. Then, after Steve had completed his master's, we turned around again and went back to Tucson.

I again enrolled at the University of Arizona, almost ready to graduate. Then I got pregnant.

In some ways, pregnancy was a big change for me. I gained 40 pounds! You'd think that with my eating issues, this would have upset me. But for some reason, I wasn't that worried. I knew pregnant women were supposed to gain weight. I just figured that I could get back down to my regular weight after the birth. And I was still running.

That didn't happen as soon as I had expected. What I mean is that Timothy was born almost a month late. If you ever want to feel really delightful, try extending a pregnancy for 3 or 4 weeks. That's as good as it gets (not)! Anyway, after the birth, I did lose the weight very quickly, just as I had planned.

My mother had also made some plans. It seemed she had decided that what I needed to keep me busy was a business. After she had sold her nursing home business in Michigan, my parents had moved to Arizona, and she purchased a travel agency in Tucson for me to run. I know she meant well; I'm sure she saw the business as a great opportunity. But I had just graduated from college, and I had a baby. I didn't need to be kept busy! And I knew nothing about the travel industry. With my help, the agency went out of business in 18 months.

This was a pretty traumatic experience for me. The backstory was that before purchasing it, we had met the man who owned the agency. He had told us that he planned to develop it into a franchise and that if we bought this agency, he would help us get it going. My mother invested the money she'd gotten from selling her own business. Instead of helping us get our feet on the ground, however, the guy basically walked away. Neither my mother nor I had a clue about how to run this kind of business, and I had zero aptitude for it. My parents lost a lot of money in the deal, and I felt completely awful. At the time, it felt like a turning point in my relationship with my parents. I felt like I had let them down.

Meanwhile, Steve and I never saw each other. I was working days at the agency and he was working the night shift at the mines. It was beginning to take a toll. The two of us were living together more like roommates than like husband and wife.

As I had understood it, the idea behind Steve's getting his master's degree was so he could get a higher salary, but he was making the same amount of money as before. Plus, the move back to Michigan had cost us a lot of money. So instead of getting ahead, we were falling behind. The only way Steve could see to make more money was to take shift work. Of course, for that, he didn't need the extra degree, so it seemed like a big waste. It also seemed that we had a basic philosophical difference: I was more "work to live" and Steve was more "live to work." I'll work as hard as anyone else as long as there seems to be a point to it, some payoff, some quality of life. We just didn't seem to be on the same wavelength.

This was not a beautiful existence. While I came by the nickname Motormouth honestly, I wasn't especially articulate or comfortable discussing emotional situations. So even though I was frustrated, I didn't know how to express it. That might well have been true of Steve, too. In any case, I looked for comfort where I had always looked for it: in athletics, in extreme physical exertion. After the travel agency adventure, I became the aerobics director at a downtown Tucson health club and was teaching aerobics again. I started to do some triathlons. Now my anorexia was kicking into high gear. I couldn't eat. I couldn't even drink water. Looking back, it's easy to guess that the stress in my marriage was becoming a real problem and, in reaction, I was creating bigger problems for myself. I finally ended up checking into the psychiatric hospital. At the time, there was no other place for someone with an eating disorder to go to for help. I can't forget the words of wisdom I received there: "When you're starving yourself, you're not thinking clearly." You can say that again.

I could see, however, that my marriage was in really bad shape. I decided to take radical action.

By ending the marriage? No, by having another child.

Having Tim had brought Steve and me closer, especially at the beginning. Steve was a really good dad. He was especially good with little kids. I thought that having a second child would help our relationship, that it might make us more united as a family. I had taken the failure of the travel agency really hard. Maybe admitting that the marriage was also a failure seemed like too much.

Looking back on those years, it doesn't really seem as if I was moving in a straight line or in a loop or even around in circles. It's more like I was in a maze. I had only a very vague idea of where I was headed, and not much more of an idea of where I wanted to go. I guess I just figured (and hoped) that at some point I'd find my way out.

[TWO]

WHERE I AM

CHAPTER 7

JIM: SEEING EYE-TO-EYE AND BUTTING HEADS

I was still working at the health club downtown when I took on another job as an aerobics instructor at the Tucson Racquet Club so I could use their pool. My second child, Andrew, had been born in April, and I used to take him to the pool with me. He'd sit strapped into his little baby seat at the side of the pool while I swam.

It was October when I first met Jim. In fact, I met Jim at the gym! The weird thing was that a woman in my aerobics class who knew I was working out with an eye toward competing in the Ironman Triathlon in Hawaii said to me, "You really should meet my husband." Yeah—you can see this story coming from a mile away. I learned later that not only was this woman telling me that I should meet her husband, she was also telling her husband that he should meet me because I was into all the same things he was into: doing triathlons and working out.

One October day, I was doing laps in the pool at the gym. As I

45

got to the end of the pool, a guy was standing over me, watching. He leaned over and introduced himself. He knew who I was, and he said that he'd been watching me swim for months, though I hadn't really noticed.

Jim was very into fitness and competing. He told me that when he was in high school in Connecticut he'd been athletic. He had gone to a prep school in Fairfield just so he could play ice hockey, but then he hadn't actually gone out for the team once he was there. After he'd gotten out of school, he turned into a couch potato and started to get fat. Then he joined an accounting firm where everyone worked out and was really fit. One guy there sold him a bike, and he started biking and running. He also joined a masters swimming program at the University of Arizona and swam every morning. Soon he was running 10-Ks and then doing short triathlons. In 1988, Jim bought a business and became a self-employed accountant. At that time, it was a seasonal tax practice, so on April 15 he could just lock the door and swim, run, and cycle to his heart's content.

When I met Jim in the fall of '89, he was obsessive-compulsive about exercising. He had just recently done his first Ironman competition. Meanwhile, if I wanted to do Ironman Hawaii—a somewhat distant but definite goal—I still needed to qualify. Jim was very emphatic about my doing the Canadian Ironman as my qualifier: There was no question in his mind that Ironman Canada should be my next step. He had done Canada and was sure it would be right for me.

That was how our relationship started. Jim was very decisive and take-charge right from the beginning, and I totally appreciated this quality. It felt good to have someone who was interested in my performance—someone who could help me focus my talent, whatever it might turn out to be. Although Steve had played a little tennis with me in high school and college, he really hadn't been that interested in it and had soon quit. He just was not especially athletically oriented, so he'd pretty much left me to do my own thing while he did his own thing.

I signed up for Ironman Canada, which was 10 months away, and Jim, planning to compete there again, suggested that we train together, riding bikes and swimming. It was an offer I found impossible to refuse. I remember that the first time we rode together I couldn't help thinking that he looked really good on a bike. The attraction was definitely there.

This was in stark contrast to the continual stress at home, where there were so many responsibilities, necessities, and chores. There were dishes to wash and laundry to fold. When I was with Jim, there was just bike riding. That may not be paradise for everyone, but for me it was really great. It was like taking a vacation from reality. Jim must have felt the same way, because within a month we had . . . what? I guess "fallen for each other" says it as well as anything else could.

Because I was spending so much time with Jim, even though there was nothing sexual in our relationship at that point, I felt very divided. I needed to talk to Steve about this. I had tried a few times to bring it up but had not been able to get Steve's attention. Finally, in my own straightforward way, I said, "We need to talk." He was watching television at the time. I felt that the tone of my voice would make him take his eyes off the screen. I was wrong.

The next day I moved out. But I didn't go flying into Jim's arms. I took both my boys—Tim was 4 and Andrew was 9 months old— and moved into an apartment near my parents' house. I think Steve was shocked that I would do something like that, so then he wanted to get counseling. But I was pissed off and determined. It seemed like I'd been trying for a long time to call it to his attention that the marriage wasn't working, so I basically said forget it.

Jim also left his wife around this time. It was tax season and he took a small apartment where he could work, near where I was living.

Although we were both away from our spouses, we weren't really together. It was a short interlude. We basically saw each other throughout tax season—again, high romance was not exactly a hallmark of my love life. Then we both got a bad case of nerves. Jim went back to his wife, and I moved back in with Steve. What a mess!

None of this is a fond memory for me. I would not advise anyone to start having an affair. In my case, it left me with some really unpleasant feelings. And it wasn't over yet. Early that summer I happened to meet Jim when we were both out riding bikes. Everything started all over again. Ironman Canada was in August, now only a couple of months away, and both of us were registered for it. So it only made sense that we should get in shape together, right?

Throughout that summer of training, I was in my element. It was so cool to have a guy with whom I could do the things I loved the most. We biked all over the Tucson area—at Saguaro National Park and also, oddly enough, on the frontage road on which, years later, I would do my 300-mile run. We rode about 60 miles three times a week—it was one of the rare times in my life when I trained for a specific competition. Jim complained about biking on the frontage road because it's relatively flat, which he claimed wouldn't sufficiently prepare us for the conditions in Canada. I whined that I didn't want to do hills because they were too tough. But for the most part we just had fun together.

The race in Canada is still one of the best experiences I've had in my life. Jim was right about the hills. But even though I'd whined about doing hills when we were training, we'd still trained very hard. I had decided that I was just going to give it my best. I had no idea what that would mean.

All the time we were training, it goes without saying that Jim was the better athlete. He could swim better, run better, and bike better. Though I was not as good as Jim, I have always been a strong swimmer, and so I did pretty well in the first part of the triathlon.

And my transition—getting out of my wet suit and onto the bike—
went well. Jim's transition wasn't so good. It wasn't until 25 miles
into the bike race that he caught up to me. Then something funny
happened. Usually, of the two of us, I was the whiner. This time, as
we were facing a big hill, Jim started complaining and swearing
about how tough it was. I thought to myself, "I can't listen to this for
112 miles!" And I just took off. I swear I didn't even notice the hills.
It was the coolest feeling.

As I approached the next transition, at about mile 110 of the bike
race, I noticed that some of the top runners were just starting. I
thought, "What's Scott Tinley doing here?" I got chills. Tinley has
won or placed in nearly all the triathlons in which he's competed;
he's now in the Ironman Hall of Fame. Then I saw Paula Newby-
Fraser and Erin Baker, the top two women in the world at that
time. I was completely overwhelmed. I realized that I was doing
amazingly well.

Then I started running. I felt like total crap. I was just really used
up and now I had a marathon to run. Even with my great start, by
mile 5 other women started passing me. Canadian Lori Bowden
started to pass me but then, all of a sudden, she went to the side of
the road and threw up. A few minutes later, she passed me again. (I
later learned that, like me, this was her first Ironman competition.
She's won a bunch of them since then.)

It's really funny how your energy level and motivation can
fluctuate during a race, and the things that give you a boost are
weird. I was feeling wrecked until a guy came up to me as I was
running along and said, "You look so good!" I thought, "Huh? I do?"
I really hadn't imagined that I did, but, well, if *he* thought I looked
good . . . that gave me more energy.

The running part of the competition was a loop course. I'd made
the turnaround and was headed toward the finish when I passed
Jim, who was still on his way out. He growled. Since ours was a new

relationship, he didn't get that mad at me for taking off without him. I know he wasn't thrilled, though.

With a time of 10 hours and 25 minutes, I ended up being the ninth woman overall, but I had been *third* in the biking part of the race. Jim did really well, too. It was his second Ironman, and he did it in 11:30. I can honestly say that it was with this race that I began to get a sense of myself as a serious athlete. This was the real beginning of my career. My personal life was a wreck, but this was something I could do.

Some runners like to get really "high" for their events. By this I mean that they go for that big adrenaline rush. They like to feel their hearts pounding. I don't like that feeling, whether it's when I'm running or in other parts of my life. After we got back from Canada, I experienced that kind of intense excitement as I snuck around to be with Jim. It did not feel at all comfortable. I knew that this was a very unreal way to live. It was unpredictable, and I knew it couldn't go on. At the same time, I knew that my marriage to Steve was not going well. So it was pretty clear what had to happen. I had to end my relationship with one man in order to stabilize my relationship with the other.

I moved out of the house for the second time. But even though Jim was "taking charge" of me, giving me advice that led to my becoming a full-time aerobics director at the Jewish Community Center, he had not dealt with his first relationship. He didn't move out, and, in fact, I discovered later that he was in the process of buying a house. When I confronted him about this, he explained that he wanted to be sure that his two kids had a home. He finally told his wife about us at Christmastime that year. It was excruciating.

By January of '91 we were finally talking about straightening ourselves out and getting married. Timing being as odd as it often is, I think I was officially divorced and remarried during the same week. Even though this was what I really wanted, it was completely nuts. We'd planned to get married in August at Lake Tahoe, California, but that fell through and we ended up at my mom's friend's house in Chicago with a justice of the peace. My parents served as witnesses. It was a very intense year. I felt like we'd put everybody through so much crap. I would *never* repeat that.

We wanted to have a second wedding ceremony at Sabino Canyon, in Tucson, with Jim's family. All of us—Jim, me, and the four boys—were living in my parents' house while my parents were in Wisconsin for the summer. The day was such a nightmare—the kids wouldn't get dressed, there was so much chaos. Lots of drama, lots of shouting. But the bottom line is that Jim and I have been married ever since.

The way in which someone meets his or her spouse is said to be very revealing. Everything that will happen in the future is supposedly foreshadowed in that first meeting. In my marriage to Jim, there seems to be some truth to that belief. For one thing, the Ironman was the original basis for our being together, and competition, in one way or another, is still really important in our lives. Jim also advised me, in no uncertain terms, of what I ought to do as an athlete—and he still does that today. He gets really aggravated if he thinks I'm doing less than my best, whether it's choosing which events to be in or performing in an individual race.

Although I was first attracted to Jim's extremely opinionated views about what I should be doing, I'm also very opinionated myself. Our views are not always in sync, to put it mildly. Obviously this adds an element of sparring to our relationship. Sometimes we just plain piss each other off.

A while back I took part in a 100-mile race in Colorado. Jim was there, and he felt that I was giving a mediocre effort. Regardless of whether I was or wasn't, this struck me as a big blast of negativity, and I dropped out of the race. Right now I don't want Jim to come to any more of my events. Lately, his being there just seems to do a lot more harm than good.

It may sound strange, but there's really nothing personal in this. In my own mind, Jim's presence at my races represents thoughts and feelings I'd rather do without. When he's not around, I'm able to completely disconnect from those thoughts. You could say I'm using him as a kind of scapegoat, but I know it helps.

As much as I was into Pam and how much fun we were having, I felt totally guilty, especially about my kids. Jonathan was a newborn; Greg was 3. This led to a false start—moving out and then moving back in. It took most of 2 years for us to finally move in together. Jonathan was 2 and Greg was 5.

The guilt got in the way of my working out. I was still doing it a lot, but less and less. Also, I was building my business, and that was taking more of my time. My "exercise addiction" waned. I was working out less and getting slower while Pam was working out more and getting faster. When I first met Pam, she was riding a clunker bike and I could *kill* her at swimming. Then the tables turned. Truthfully, I was envious.

Then a client, Benny Linkhart, bought me a subscription to *UltraRunning* magazine—the Bible for the sport, even today. Pam and I looked at the magazine and got excited; we thought it would be fun to try an ultra. We picked the Elkhorn 100-K (62 miles) in Helena, Montana. Since the Elkhorn race would be hilly and mountainous, we decided to go to Jackson, Wyoming, a place I've loved for years, to do some long-distance running there. In these early years, we could leave the kids with our former spouses when we went away. (My two live with their mom in any case.) So we were able to make a little vacation of it.

Since neither of us really knew what we were getting into, we made a pact to stay together for the whole race. It took us 14 or 15 hours to complete the course, but we stayed together. At the end, my feet were like hamburger— I could hardly walk. Pam was fine. I probably should have known right then that this was her thing, not mine.

Then we decided to do a 100-mile race, the Wasatch Front 100 at Salt Lake. Again, we agreed to run together. And again, at around mile 60, my feet gave up—and my attitude began to get negative. For a while, I kept telling Pam it was okay if she wanted to go on ahead without me. Finally, we came to the base of a big hill. I said again that, *really*, it was okay if she wanted to go on ahead. She went right up that hill like she was running from the cops or something! I thought, "Oh, gee, Pam, was I holding you back?" I had said to go ahead, but then I couldn't accept it when she did.

Later, it bothered me even more when she'd say something like "I'm going to run with you for the first 20 miles," but then at mile 2 some lady would pass her and she'd forget all about me and take off.

For myself, I don't care about winning. But I do want Pam to know that we're a team here. I've helped her with every aspect of her career.

—*Jim Reed*

At the same time, there are certain things that Jim is much more positive and adventurous about than I am. He's a risk taker, and he's been able to take me with him to a lot of places I wouldn't have gone by myself. The truth is that I probably never would have become an ultrarunner at all without Jim. He got me to be serious about triathlons, which is how my ultrarunning started. This has been true in so many areas of our life together. Right now we have a home in Tucson and another in Jackson Hole, Wyoming. Jim has been able to make this happen through a combination of hard work and fearlessness. If it had been up to me, I would have hesitated (maybe forever) about getting a second home. He just went for it. I really benefit from being with someone who's aggressive in that way.

One thing that Jim and I have in common, I think, is that when the pressure is on to get something done, we can do it. I remember one time when we literally had only about 4 hours to move *everything* out of a house we'd been living in. By ourselves. And somehow, we did it. Of course, I'm not saying that we weren't screaming at each other the entire time!

I want to be really frank about our marriage. For one thing, I don't want this to be a book that's just about my running. Running can't be separated from the other things that are going on with me, especially in my closest relationships. Also, I think people know that marriages are really a lot more complicated than they are depicted to be, especially marriages that involve not just one athlete but two. When you put a couple of very competitive people in a house together, you're going to have some drama. You're going to have people using one another to motivate themselves, to convince themselves of things they can or can't do, and to blame one another for things they feel guilty about. On the flip side, you'll also see how two people can make each other better and stronger even while they're pulling on the rope in opposite directions. That really can happen, as long as the two of you keep pulling. It's when one stops that you both hit the dirt.

I once talked with a woman who believed she could never be a good runner. She said, "I've tried it, but the whole time I was running, all I could think was, 'When will I get to stop?'" And I thought, "I feel that way lots of times, and I just keep going." Maybe it's the same way with marriage, or at least some marriages. You just want to hang in there and finish the race. As someone who made the decision to end a marriage, I think it's really a matter of taking responsibility, of owning the commitment you *choose* to make, rather than anything you *have* to do. It's a very individual thing, what is comfortable (or tolerable) for people. Believe it or not, it's that way with running, too. You may have to drop out of a race because of pain or injury, but another person could have a more painful injury and keep going.

To some, comparing marriage to a difficult long-distance run might seem like a bleak view. For me, it doesn't feel depressing. It's just everyday reality. It's what I'm used to. And to be honest, it's what works for me. I honestly don't believe any marriage is paradise.

CHAPTER 8

I DON'T WANT
TO BE SICK

One of the first things Jim and I did was buy a house—a real fixer-upper, otherwise known as a total dump. Right away, we set to work gutting it almost entirely. We took out floors and busted up and removed tile. We pulled out the entire kitchen. I think the only thing we left was one bathtub. In more ways than one, our marriage began with demolition.

I was starting to have a lot of trouble with my not-eating problem. Steve had just never gotten it, but with my mother's help I had checked into the psychiatric hospital for treatment once. Obviously there had been no miracle cure. During my two pregnancies, I'd gained weight as I was supposed to, but I'd dropped it right away. I also had what I now think could have been postpartum depression after the birth of each of my sons. During those times, I simply could not get along with my mother at all. I'm sure that it also affected my relationship with Steve.

Then, separating from Steve, the divorce, and marriage to Jim—it was all so much. Meanwhile, I just went along acting like everything was fine. I kept running, doing races, and not eating. I was getting sicker and sicker, but I don't think it was obvious to others. At the time I was working as a personal trainer for a few women. One of them was the owner of a local "retreat," a fancy combination rest and rehab facility called Sierra Tucson. I told her about the trouble I was having, and she encouraged me to sign in for a 6-week stay. It was not exactly affordable, but between a gift from my parents and Jim and me making up the rest, I was able to swing it.

Because I was really good at functioning without eating anything, I think it was hard for Jim to see my condition as serious. But he totally supported me when I checked into Sierra Tucson right after we were married, leaving him with four boys to look after on his own.

While I languished in forced inactivity, Jim not only cared for the kids but also oversaw the remodeling of the house. He hired a couple of his clients to do the plastering and put in new wood floors and tile. All the changes gave me something to look forward to when I was able to come home.

I certainly couldn't complain about my accommodations. Situated at the base of the Santa Catalina Mountains, what was at that time Sierra Tucson is today Miraval, one of the best spas in the country, blessed with Oprah Winfrey's seal of approval. Whatever else it may be, at this kind of hospital, life is supposed to be simplified. Nobody expects you to do all the things that you usually do—you don't have to shop, you don't have to cook or clean, you don't have to work. In fact, you *can't* do those things even if you want to. All you have to do—all you're allowed to do—is focus on the problem that brought you there. With the hassles of everyday life eliminated, your problem can be more effectively understood and dealt with. That's the theory.

This particular hospital served a mixture of purposes. Some people checked in just to de-stress. In fact, Jim had spent a couple of weeks there during our affair, when he was still married. I could certainly understand him wanting to de-stress from that! The hospital also treated all kinds of addictions—drug addiction, alcoholism, sex addiction—and it had an entire wing devoted to eating disorders. A large percentage of the counselors and other staff seemed to be former addicts themselves.

I am certain that this second hospitalization did help me with my anorexia. I'm also certain that the help didn't come in the way the staff intended.

The tranquilized environment of a psychiatric hospital surely benefits many people. This place was out in the sticks, away from pretty much everything. For someone who is totally stressed out, it must be a great relief to be in an environment where stress is never allowed to raise its ugly head. For me, there was a basic flaw in the system. As a business major in college, I had been introduced to the principle of economics (and human nature) known as Parkinson's Law: "Work expands so as to fill the time available for its completion." If, for example, I have 9 months to take care of all my responsibilities as race director of the Tucson Marathon, I will still wind up doing some things at the last minute—just as I would if I'd had 6 months, or 3 months. I found that psychological problems, too, can expand to fill the available time, no matter how much time that might be. Having all day to think and talk about anorexia can magnify the problem instead of helping to bring it under control. At least that was my experience. My anorexia didn't get worse while I was in the hospital, but it did loom larger.

To understand what being in the hospital was like, imagine being in a place where all you can do is watch television. Then imagine that the same program is on every channel: "Welcome once again to *The Anorexia Show!*"

Anorexia here, anorexia there, anorexia everywhere! I was called upon to look at my problem from every possible angle. Sometimes my running was brought into this, sometimes it wasn't. Did I run to justify eating something? Or did I run to prevent myself from eating? Did I run to gain a sense of control over my life, or to escape a sense of being controlled by others? Some of the theories that were batted around were extremely far-fetched. For instance, was I sexually abused as a child? Did my failure to recall any sexual abuse mean that it hadn't taken place? Or did it prove that abuse *had* taken place but was too traumatic for me to consciously remember? Although for me this was *so* not an issue, I was called upon to cover the potential causes of my eating disorder from all angles. Believe me, exploring all the possibilities can really fill up the day.

This was in 1992, at the very beginning of the Prozac era, and I was prescribed this wonder drug as part of my treatment. I pretended to swallow the pills, but I threw them away. I'm just not a pill taker. I have to practically be dying before I'll take even an aspirin.

At Sierra Tucson, my caloric intake was strictly monitored. I assume that the protocols were based on the behavior of bulimics rather than anorexics, because bread and pasta were prohibited on the theory that they would lead to bingeing. I was kept to 1,200 calories per day, to be gotten mostly, it seemed at the time, from spaghetti squash, a vegetable I'd never seen before.

And exercise was forbidden. Despite that, it wasn't long before I was doing situps in my room. And I discovered that it wasn't hard to sneak out and go running on the trails around the hospital. In fact, one night I called Jim and told him to pick me up on a road a short way from Sierra. It was like we were high school kids sneaking out of the house after curfew. He took me home, where I got to see all the work that had been done, and we had a really nice evening together. Then he took me back to the hospital so I could sneak back in. After all, we were newlyweds, remember!

I'm not trying to make light of this experience, and I don't mean to imply that I didn't need help. I was having some very dangerous and deluded ideas. Somehow, anorexia had hooked into my competitive nature. When I was in high school, I had turned not eating into a game. I thought I could put one over on everyone. I had all kinds of little techniques and tricks to make people think I was eating. Now, I was a parent. I wasn't in control of the game. I knew it was out of control—the game was beating me.

What finally helped me was not the hospital's empty days or endless therapies. What helped was seeing women who had actually taken their weight down to 70 pounds. They were a shocking sight: Women who looked like concentration camp prisoners but honestly believed they were *fat*. Their self-images were completely distorted. At least I *knew* that I was too thin. These women were really sick and had no control over their condition. I couldn't and wouldn't allow myself to go down that path. If, as the doctors suggested, my anorexia was part of an unconscious process, the sight of these terribly ill people sent a message that somehow got through to me at the deepest possible level. The message was: You've taken this pretty far, but you're not going to take it any farther. So back off.

At that point, I may not have been cured, but I had definitely woken up. I left the hospital after 4 of the 6 weeks.

Over the years, a lot of people who have learned that I've had anorexia have said, "Oh, I get it—now you run. You've got an addictive personality, and you've just given up one addiction for another one." I think they really miss the point. I've thought about this a lot, and this is how I see it: I didn't stop eating because of any special aversion to food. It's true that I didn't care very much about food in the first place and that I was put off by the physical changes I saw my friends going through during adolescence. But it was really about being competitive. At the time my anorexia began, I wanted to be the best gymnast I could possibly be. I didn't care about running then. The two things—not eating and running—had nothing to do with one another. It was about having the ideal gymnast's body.

Later, I wanted to play tennis. I had some talent and wanted to be the best I could be. That's when I started running more—not for its own sake, and not in connection with the anorexia. At that point, the anorexia was already established. It had started out as one thing, and then it just became part of who I was. It didn't seem to interfere with my tennis game, so I wasn't that worried about it.

It wasn't until a good while afterward that I began to do races, triathlons, Ironman competitions, and eventually ultras, and I realized that I had a real talent for running. I wanted to be the best at *that*. By then the anorexia had developed a mind of its own. It was a serious problem, one that I couldn't see any way of solving. I couldn't just quit having it. And it wasn't helping me to be competitive anymore. In fact, it kept me from fulfilling my running goals. Once I registered that, I knew I had to take control again. If I was going to be competitive, I had to eat.

Since then, I've developed healthier eating behaviors so I'll have the physical strength and stamina required for long endurance races. If I hadn't addressed it, anorexia could have ended my running career.

What's ironic is that I think anorexia may also have helped me as an athlete because of the unique demands of my sport. Not eating was an illness that over the years conditioned my body to function on minimal nourishment. I unintentionally had been simulating the conditions of a 100-mile run every day of my life.

Maybe I do have an addictive personality. If so, I'm addicted to wanting to do my best every day.

CHAPTER 9

MY BRAIN, PART TWO:
OF MICE AND ME

I t's been said that if life is a race, it's a marathon rather than a sprint. That's definitely how it seems to me, and it's a marathon that's run every day. I do all the things that millions of other "married with children" women do. I go to the supermarket, run the washing machine, prepare meals, feed the dog, drive the kids wherever they need to go. I also run a business—the Tucson Marathon—that takes up more of my time as the December race date approaches. On top of this, I manage to run for at least 3 hours every day.

While nobody's forcing me to do this, it's not really a choice, either. There's something in my nature that makes it really hard for me to sit still.

When I was in the hospital for anorexia, I took part in many group therapy as well as individual counseling sessions. Pretty much everything about my life was discussed and analyzed. My running, while not generating as much interest as I had expected, was seen as an aspect of the illness that had brought me to the hospital. Since I obviously was sick, maybe running was part of my illness. Was it an addiction? Was it compulsive behavior? What was I running away from? Or was I running toward something?

Maybe a few thought on this will be of help to other runners or anorexics.

To a lot of people, long-distance running seems to signify some kind of personality disorder. Maybe it's because most people are not in good physical condition. To someone who's out of shape, running can be painful, so the idea that anyone would deliberately choose to inflict that pain upon themselves may seem self-destructive.

If you're not only in good physical condition but also temperamentally suited to running, the situation is different. Running is something you're ready to do, something you want to do, and perhaps even something you're *born* to do.

Seriously, no one would stand next to Shaquille O'Neal and ask him why he plays basketball. The attributes that make up a runner are not always as obvious as the height of a basketball player. Yet they're just as important, from the runner's point of view. When Shaq tries to get into a car or sleep in a standard-size bed, the fact that he's more than 7 feet tall can be a drawback. That same fact can be a big help when he's on the basketball court. In the same way, being temperamentally attuned to perpetual motion makes me pretty uncomfortable on long car trips or in sedate social settings. In the middle of a long run, I'm *more* comfortable than I am just about anywhere else.

In a study at the University of Wisconsin, two groups of mice spent several hours a day running on treadmills. The mice in one group had been bred over six generations for running ability and motivation. In the other group were just regular mice. After each running session, the researchers measured the brain activity of all the mice, which showed that all of them were mentally stimulated by the exercise. Next, the mice bred for running were denied access to the treadmill while the others had their daily workout. When the mice's brain activity was measured again, the researchers expected to find evidence of stimulation in the mice who had done the running. And that is what they found. The scientists also expected that the "racing mice," who had not been allowed to run, would be more subdued than usual. However, it turned out that the running mice were *overstimulated* by the inactivity. Not running made them uncomfortable, or even frantic, because running was what they had been born and bred to do. Running actually calmed them. I don't really want to compare myself to rodents, but I empathize with those racing mice.

• • • • •

Sometimes running is described as an addiction. (A major manufacturer even calls one of its running shoe models *Addiction 6!*) I don't think this is accurate, but I've heard it so often that it deserves to be addressed.

Addiction is defined in a variety of ways and can be both physical and emotional. There are also various "symptoms" that are considered to be indicators of addiction. For a start, guilt is supposed to be a basic element. Even though guilt is usually considered an unpleasant feeling, among addicts, guilt is an essential part of the "rush." If the guilt is taken away, the addiction loses some of its power.

Well, it is true that there are times when I feel guilty about taking as much time as I do to run. I'm aware that running has sometimes taken me away from my family, and I'm concerned about that. But there's definitely no excitement for me in those feelings. It's not the kind of guilt that has a "rush" to it, as there might be if running were some forbidden pleasure. There's certainly nothing secret about my running. I've never been a secretive person, and the few times I have done things surreptitiously I definitely didn't like it.

Also, although I wish I could be everything for everybody all the time, I recognize that it's just not possible to be a perfect wife, mother, and international athlete. Wonder Woman is a comic book character; she doesn't live in Tucson, Arizona, or anywhere else in the real world. So my guilt in regard to running is relatively limited.

Another basic psychological theory is that addiction is defined by the severity of the withdrawal symptoms someone experiences when the object of the addiction is taken away. When people are addicted to drugs, for example, the pain they feel when drug administration is stopped is a measure of their addiction's strength.

Does that mean that a mother who grieves over the loss of her children is addicted to them? That a violinist devastated by an inability to play is an addict? I don't think it's helpful to attach a single label, especially a very negative one, to a range of human activities. I'm sure it's possible that someone who runs as much as I do could do so as an expression of a mental or emotional problem. That diagnosis needs to be made one person at a time. As for me, I may have problems, but running isn't one of them. On the contrary, I think running is my solution.

On a purely biological level, there may be some validity to the idea of running as addiction. Any intense physical activity causes the production of chemicals—endorphins—that limit pain and can be very energizing. Endorphins can give you a real buzz: the so-called runner's high. It's true that distance runners get used to endorphins. If I don't run, I feel tired. So you could say that I'm addicted to endorphins. Looking at it in a positive way, if I'm really tired, a run refreshes me.

When I'm running I can think more clearly; I can relax; I feel less stressed out or anxious. Is it an addiction to want to be focused and relaxed?

As time goes on, the runner's high can become harder and harder to obtain. I do still get it, but not in the same way that I used to. Sometimes hitting that groove takes way too long and I can be tempted to quit for the day before it hits.

And anyone who runs longer distances will more than likely experience occasional pain of some kind. This might be minor, but it can make you wonder where the "high" went. If you are running primarily to get that euphoric feeling, you have to find another reason to run.

Thankfully, I am extremely healthy. I rarely get sick, and I don't take any medication. My whole family has high blood pressure, except for me. I might exhaust myself on a long run, but I bounce back. I once ran a 135-mile race and then, the following week, I ran a 109-mile race. I seldom get even minor injuries, and I've never been seriously injured.

A final criterion of addiction is one trait that seems to separate truly addictive personalities from those with less serious compulsions: When asked, "If pushing a magic button could forever eliminate your desire for your addictive substance or activity, would you push that button?," deeply addicted people always answer yes. Obviously, if you could get rid of something that was ruining your life, you would choose to do that.

If I were asked that same question about running, I would definitely answer no. I love this. I would not want to have a life in which I wasn't able to do my sport or did not have the desire to take part in it.

CHAPTER 10

PARENTHOOD

Especially at the top levels, running is more than a matter of physical conditioning. My 45th birthday has come and gone, so obviously my performance is affected by how my aging body feels. Even more important now, however, is what's going through my mind. When things are going well, I'm able to focus on the mechanics of the race, whether I'm getting the right amounts of food and water, and who's in front of or behind me. But it's not always that way.

What should I call it when I'm thinking about my family during a run? I don't want to say it's a "distraction," because that implies that running is more important to me. But I don't know another word that describes something that makes it so difficult to concentrate. And concentration is not getting any easier. Jim's boys, who used to come around quite a lot even though they lived with their mother, started showing up less frequently once they hit high school, so they don't really occupy my mind as much as my own sons do. But all the kids are growing up and getting more complicated. Even the youngest, Jackson, who was born in 1995, is not a small child anymore. When they (and I) were younger, I used to be able to detach from all of the day-to-day crap. Now it's hard to do that.

In a way, being preoccupied gives me energy. The drawback is that it's nervous energy. I want to run as much as ever, but sometimes it may be for the wrong reason. I'm trying to burn off the feeling of not being able to relax. I'm always thinking, "Is there somewhere I'm supposed to drive somebody? Is there something I'm supposed to buy? Is there somebody I'm supposed to call?"

Being a mom has never stopped me from running, and I'm sure it never will. If I keep getting "distracted," I won't like it, but I'll deal with it. I never stopped running during my three pregnancies and I ran within a few days after each birth, even though all three deliveries were by C-section. Right about here, I should put in one of those disclaimers: *Don't try this at home.* Believe me, I realize that this is not what doctors recommend. This is just "Pam."

After the disclaimer, I guess, comes the commercial. This one is for *jogging strollers.*

Because I started to run again so soon after delivering, I discovered some pretty cool techniques for using a jogging stroller. This device is fabulous! If you've never used one, you might think that it would be awkward or even heavy. Actually, it's so well engineered that you can literally push it with your fingertips. I love this invention. I took my kids everywhere and didn't have to give up my running time.

As I ran, I kind of leaned into the stroller for support—sort of like the way you cheat on a stairclimber by holding on to the handrails to support a lot of your weight on your arms instead of on your legs. I actually used my upper body to run. I tried really hard not to bounce the baby up and down. I worked at keeping a really level stride, with my feet just barely clearing the ground. I also tried to make my landings with as little sound as possible. Once I got used to it, I found that I could even go fast like this.

Also, you fatigue much less quickly when you don't lift your legs high at the knees.

I have to say that running with my kids like this was really a joy. It's how I bonded with my boys. When Tim was a baby, he was colicky. He was in pain—his tummy hurt—and so he would scream and cry. I'd put him in the stroller and go for a run. Otherwise, he would have driven me nuts. I mean, I felt *bad* for him, but after a while ... *aye yi yi!*

When Andrew was born I got a double stroller, and all three of us would go for a run. It was so much fun. I'd sing and make them sing with me. Tim would hit Andrew over the head and Andrew would cry—great bonding. I'd talk and make them listen to me. This worked for a while, until they got a little older and said, "Mom, shut up!" Anyway, it was good, really fun, and it lasted until each of them was about 5 years old. Those were some of the best times of my life.

As the kids got older, I couldn't really rely on the baby jogger to serve as babysitter. The boys had to get to school or to activities. There was a lot more to manage. People ask me how, having kids, I can go on an 8 or 10-hour training run. The answer is that I can't. I have to break up my training into smaller bits throughout the day.

I get up very early, usually around 4:00 or 4:30 in the morning. By 6:00, I've run my first 6 miles before feeding the kids and getting them off to school. Then I do another 6 miles, often with our Old English sheepdog, Aspen. Next, if it's "marathon season"—which includes a good part of the year but gets really crazy during the late summer and fall—I work on Tucson Marathon business. Otherwise, there are all the usual household chores. I run another 6 miles in the early afternoon before going to get the kids and take them wherever they need to go, depending on what day it is and what is planned. Once I have them situated, I can run another 6 miles before thinking about dinner and anything else I need to take care of. Now that the kids are old enough to stay home by themselves, I often feed Jackson and Andrew, and then Jim and I go out for dinner together. Being able to sit across the table from each other, without having to jump up to serve or clear, gives us a chance to catch up. Tucson's restaurants see a lot of us.

We don't live like other people. We don't do dinner or church. We're domestically challenged. —*Tim Koski*

We usually don't sit down together as a family. Mom feeds Jackson and me and then she and Jim go out to eat. We're all doing our own thing. I like it this way. —*Andrew Koski*

I'd forgo dinner for skiing any day. —*Tim*

Dinners are not the focus. —*Andrew*

Even at Thanksgiving we leave Mom in Tucson to work on the marathon and we go to Wyoming and go skiing. —*Tim*

I remember one Christmas, when our dinner was turkey and popcorn. No, I think it was pretzels. Something weird. French fries—turkey and French fries. It was really ghetto. But we're all close. Well, semiclose. —*Andrew*

She's a good mom. She helps out and makes dinner for everyone. And she cleans up after us. —*Jackson Reed*

You pay a price when you try to excel at too many things. Some people who do well in their careers wind up trashing their families. That's putting it very bluntly, and I don't mean to speak ill of anyone. I guess what I mean is that there can often be an element of neglect, or at least seeming neglect, and families are strained or even broken by it. It's not hard to understand why that happens. In order to truly excel at anything, especially athletics, you have to devote a tremendous amount of time to it. Since raising a family also takes a lot of time, choices are made, either consciously or unconsciously. Sometimes people recognize what's happening in their lives and try to keep control, and other times things just happen by themselves.

I feel the strain most when I have to leave to do an event somewhere away from home. Frequently there is a conflict with something else that needs attention, whether it's a family occasion or something for school or for Jim's work. I feel guilty, really terrible, and sometimes I don't even want to go. This started when my kids were born, so it's been like this for a long time. It's only because I can tell myself that I'm performing at the top level of my sport, that I really do have something to offer it, that I can let go of this feeling— at least enough so that it's not crippling while I'm competing.

It's a blessing when she's gone [to a race]. There's nobody telling you what to do.

—*Andrew Koski*

There's just always something going on. I suppose another option would have been not to have a family at all. Some of the top ultrarunners don't have children. Other talented athletes make the decision to put their families first and simply stop competing. Someone who wanted to be an Olympic swimmer might now do laps at the Y once or twice a week. Is that sad, or is it just growing up?

I'm not a recreational runner. Physically and mentally, I'm not much different from the way I was before I became a mother. I'm still doing the same things and thinking about the same goals. I've chosen an athlete's life, but a lot of guilt goes along with it. Recently we were in Wyoming doing some work on our new home. Because Andrew and Jackson were in school, Tim was staying with them in Tucson so they wouldn't miss classes. I missed a parent-teacher conference at Jackson's school. We did make it up, but missing the scheduled date without a good excuse such as an emergency was frowned upon. I know that as a mom I get trashed for that, that I'm not considered to be a good parent. I'm raising my children, but I'm still a child myself in the sense that kids tend to put themselves first.

• • • • •

Right now, a big question is where we are going to live full-time. Jim likes Wyoming. The boys like Tucson. I can run in either place, so for me the deciding factor is that I do not want to take my teenager out of his high school. I don't think it's fair to do that. And Jim knows this, too. His family moved from Connecticut to Arizona when he was a senior in high school. It's hard to get your bearings when you suddenly are in a different place and you don't have the friends or routine you grew up with. I know Jim was really lonely—that may be part of the reason he got married the first time, in college, when he was just 18 years old.

I can see in my relationship with my kids some of the same dynamic that was present in my own family when I was growing up. Like my parents, I am not much of a hugger. But my kids mean everything to me, so when they were small, it was easy to hug them. As they got older—maybe because they're boys—they seemed to want the physical affection much less. Now, ironically, I want to give them hugs and they don't want to be hugged. It hurts me, but that's the way I was, and it's the way they are.

I think one thing Jim and I agree on is that kids need to do their own homework. Lots of parents practically do the work for their kids. I want my boys to figure it out. That's real life. I will answer the occasional question, but I'm not going to sit down every night to make sure their homework is done, with every answer right. That's the boys' responsibility. They are really independent—even Jackson is very independent.

Mom makes me do chores and stuff. Our family isn't lazy.

—*Jackson Reed*

On the other hand, I don't want them to have to be adults too quickly. Jim would say that I am bad about "the money thing," that I give them anything they ask for. My feeling is that what's ours is theirs. Work is something that they'll have to do for the rest of their lives, so why rush it? Andrew was working at a pizza place. It was just a part-time job, but I asked, "Oh, is this too much for you?" Jim said, "Nah, it's good for him. He has his own money." That's something Jim and I argue about. Maybe there's a balance.

I like that the kids are involved in lots of different sports. Tim played baseball all through high school. He skis, he fly-fishes, he does some rock climbing. Andrew is extremely athletic. He could be really good at any sport he got serious about. He plays football. He also likes to ski. Jackson plays soccer and baseball. The one thing that gets me is how everything has to be organized for kids now. I mean, kids should be able to keep themselves amused, to play by themselves. These days, if it isn't organized for them, they don't want to do it. It's a real struggle for parents. I can see why some people send their kids to camp! The third time I was running at Badwater, just before going to Death Valley our family was in Jackson, where I was trying to get myself mentally focused on the upcoming race. The kids would not even go out of the house unless I pushed them out myself. It went beyond "suggesting"; I practically had to *make* them go out to play. It was like I was the camp counselor. There we were, right in the middle of Wyoming's Grand Tetons— they should have been able to find *something* to do.

Without Mom having dragged me out all the time when I was younger (I just mostly wanted to sit around and play video games), I don't know if I'd be doing the things I do now. Because of her, I go out and trail run a lot. Once you get like 5 miles out, you get away from all the people. It's a whole different world in the mountains. But I only like to run for maybe 2 or 3 hours max. I would never do 100-plus miles.

—*Tim Koski*

Of course, a *car* changes everything. Now Tim has his own car. He can take himself anywhere he wants to go without me having to chauffeur. He works, he runs, he golfs, he fly-fishes. *Aahhh!*

• • • • •

Sometimes when I'm worried that my running is taking time away from my family, people try to reassure me and say, "Oh, Pam, you're a good parent. You're a great mom." It's a nice thought that doesn't always make me feel that much better. "Good" seems like such an absolute concept. In tennis, a serve is either in or out, good or not good. In contrast, being a parent is an endless succession of gray areas. If we're going to talk about being good at something, we have to talk about being good compared to what. Am I good in terms of what I have the ability to be? I hope so. What I *want* to be? Maybe. What I *ought* to be? Maybe not.

Instead of talking about being a "good" parent, it might be better to talk about being "good enough." I think a lot of people are good enough, even if they're not really good. You don't have to win. You just have to qualify. You don't have to be the best. Just don't be the worst. That seems attainable.

I realize that as I write about parenting, I instinctively compare it to sports. Athletics and running are such big parts of my identity that I probably see everything from the perspective of marathons and ultra events. As the old saying goes, "If all you've got is a hammer, everything looks like a nail." But I do think there are ways in which being a parent really is like being in a long race.

Both, for example, can be unbearably tedious and amazingly tense at the same time. Whatever else you can say about it, running is always putting one foot in front of the other, thousands and thousands of times. You can't think about each and every step, and if you tried, you'd quickly go nuts. So you just keep making it happen for as long as it takes. At the same time, you have to be alert. You have to pay attention to your form and be aware of how you're feeling. It's being engaged and detached at the same time.

It's the same way with children. The feedings, the diaper changes, the clothes shopping, the vaccinations, making the lunches, driving them here, driving them there, day after day and year after year, like the strides of a long race. To some extent it all happens by itself—but you can never totally go on automatic pilot. Because if you do, "they" will pick up on it and find a way to get your attention. If you zone out during a run, you may have a disappointing time. With kids, on the other hand, you can wind up with a real mess, both literally and figuratively.

Running and raising kids can be boring and nerve-racking at the same time, and both also go tediously slowly and incredibly fast. Even though I've done it now more times than I can remember, when I start thinking about running 50 or 100 miles, it seems like a long way—and it *is* a long way. Then I start running. Almost always, within the first few hours, a moment comes when I feel like I've made a huge mistake: "Pam, what were you thinking?!" But I keep going. Then time starts playing some really amazing tricks. It goes slow and fast at the same time. Although I never ask how long I've been running—and I never look at my watch even though, for some perverse reason, I always wear it—I do think about how much time has passed and how much is left. This is where it gets weird. Sometimes, at the same time that it seems as if I've been running forever, it also seems like time is passing incredibly quickly. Then I think that I've got to make the best use of every possible moment.

Then, all of a sudden, the race is over. As slowly as it seemed to be going, it also seems like it was over in a flash. Hours of pain and fatigue are compressed into a single snapshot in my memory.

The same thing happens with kids, except it's not hours passing, it's years. There are endless stretches of time during which kids don't seem to change at all. They're bundles of need that only I can satisfy. It's like having a demanding, thankless boss—or several bosses, in my case. It seems like this goes on forever—until *surprise!*—it's all changed. I can't believe that my son Timothy is 21 years old. How did it happen? When did it happen? They're the same contradictory feelings I get after a long run—"too much" and "not enough" all at once—but much more powerful, and much more puzzling.

CHAPTER 11

THE TUCSON
MARATHON

When I was in high school, my mother suggested that I try working at the nursing home that she managed. My sister, Debbie, was already well established there—she started working in the kitchen and then became a nurse's aide. It was decided that I should start in the office. I lasted 2 weeks. I am not at all cut out for stay-in-one-place work.

Later, I'd gone on to get my business degree from the University of Arizona. And then there was the ill-fated travel agency. That was not a success for me either. So often, people would say to me, "Pam, if you could just take all that energy you have and put it into something useful . . ."

These days, as I've mentioned, Jim has ideas about what I should be doing. Most of the time, he is right on. That doesn't keep me from resisting his ideas when he first comes up with them. He used to have a lot of ideas about businesses I could go into for myself—

he's very entrepreneurial—and finally he had an idea that clicked with me.

Jim's great idea was that I should put on a marathon in Tucson. Up until 1993, the Tucson chapter of the Road Runners Club of America, of which Jim was the treasurer, had had a marathon that attracted around 150 competitors each year. I'm not sure why, but in '94 they didn't hold the race. So it did seem like there was an opportunity there. I could take something I was good at and turn it into something that was useful—and maybe even profitable.

Of course, I couldn't do it alone. Who could help?

My friend Pat Lekacz is a great "outside person." When I was aerobics director at Tucson's Jewish Community Center (JCC), I hired her as an instructor. She had moved to Tucson from Houston, where she worked in marketing at IBM. Pat is a dynamo with tons of energy. She's so smart, and I'm sure she could be a top executive anywhere she wanted to be, if only her family didn't move around so much. She's superdedicated to her family, which often relocates to accommodate her husband's newest business idea. She was only in Tucson for a few years before the family moved back to Houston; then she was in England for a while, and then Chicago. Anyway, Pat is very good with communications, and she wrote a lot of letters that got us meetings with potential sponsors. She also managed to organize a running expo that has become a major part of the marathon event.

Another friend, Elisa Kinder, who is also an excellent marketer, has a master's degree from Stanford. She retired at the age of 40 after a high-powered career as a Pacific Bell executive. Around 1992, Jim was trying to get me to go with him to the Road Runners Club board meetings. He kept telling me that he wanted me to meet a really cool woman who attended the meetings, but I always put him off. Sitting in a meeting just didn't sound like much fun to me.

At the time, as part of my work for the JCC, I was the race director of a duathlon. During the cycling part of the 1992 race, there was a horrible incident. The competitors had to cross a street, and the sheriff who was directing traffic told one woman that it was clear and she could go ahead. When she did, a car smacked right into her. Even though the car hit her bike, not her, she fell, hit her head, and lost consciousness. The ambulance came and took her to the hospital. It was terrible. I felt just awful. I soon learned the name of the injured woman: Elisa Kinder. One way or another, the two of us obviously were destined to meet.

I kept calling her to see if she was okay, because I was really worried. Finally, I heard back from her. We talked and decided to get together for coffee. Who would have guessed that this person who was literally run down during a race I had organized would turn out to be one of my best friends? Well, maybe Jim, who had been trying to bring us together for some time.

Elisa has become not only one of my closest friends and business partners but also a running companion. She ran with me when Jackson was a baby rolling along in the jogging stroller. Also, we're both dog runners. I run with my dog, Aspen, usually three times a day. Elisa runs with her Doberman, Sabrina—her male, Duke, is not friendly with other dogs, so he has to stay home. Elisa has been running since 1984, when she was working at the Los Angeles Olympic Games and was standing in the second row when Mary Decker fell during the 3,000-meter final. As Elisa tells it, she got mad that Decker cried about the fall. She thought, "That's not what a strong athlete would do." In some weird way, this made her want to run. She's never run a marathon—she doesn't want to risk an injury that might keep her from running anymore—but she enjoys doing shorter races. She races to compete, not against other runners, but against herself and the clock.

As one of my Tucson Marathon colleagues, Elisa initially did a bit of everything—lots of logistics, setting up, cleaning up, the works. When Pat headed back to Houston, 4 years after our startup, Elisa essentially became the head of marketing.

We also had help from Mary Croft, who recruits and coordinates our volunteers. It's a huge job—we need about 200 people for the 2-day expo before the race and many more on race day to hand out water, keep time along the course, cheer the runners on, and other important jobs, large and small, including cleaning up the course after everything's done. Mary is amazing. She's a retired nurse, and she's run at least one marathon in each of the 50 states!

Last, but by no means least, is my friend Dr. Rich Gerhauser, who is the physician for Canyon Ranch spa in Tucson and serves as the race's medical director. We always pray that we won't need his services.

I can't write a chapter about the Tucson Marathon without mentioning another special person, Mike Kasser. Mike is our biggest and most constant sponsor; in fact, the marathon is named after his commercial real estate company, Holualoa. The marathon's official name is the Holualoa Tucson Marathon. He's from Kona, Hawaii, where the Ironman Triathlon originated. Now a fit 65, Mike used to do a lot of marathons. I'm not sure what other credits he may have, but I know he's done the London and Boston Marathons back-to-back, with sub-3-hour times in each race. That is impressive. I think Mike deals with the same problem that Jim has—it's hard to be really good at your business and keep up with athletic goals at the same time. We are grateful that his love of athletics has made him want to sponsor the marathon (he sponsors my own career, too), and we wouldn't like to try to get along without him.

I can't say often enough how lucky I have been to always be surrounded by amazing people who have devoted their energy to the things I love. With the marathon, my colleagues' efforts allow me to be the official running guru. I deal with the course issues and the million and one things that it takes to get thousands of people through a 26-mile event. And it very quickly became thousands of people. There were exactly 1,200 competitors in the first race, and lately we've had between 3,500 and 4,000.

A few years before the first marathon, in 1995, Biosphere 2, a large, self-contained experimental ecological system, had been built right outside of town. The brainchild of some rich Texan, Biosphere 2 was supposed to show how people could live in perfect atmospheric balance with plants, with the plants making enough air for the people to breathe. The Biosphere people were interested in ways to draw attention to the project, and we were looking for sponsors. It was a mutually beneficial situation. We thought the course could begin at the Biosphere—an architecturally stunning building at a dramatic site—and finish in downtown Tucson. Because that distance wasn't exactly right, we had to add some twists and turns, but Biosphere 2 to downtown was the original course.

The first running was in January, but we decided we'd rather have the marathon in December. If we'd waited to schedule it for December of the following year, there would have been almost 2 years between marathons. So we did a second marathon in the same year. It seems really crazy now, but it did give some runners who had not yet qualified for Boston one last shot at it. Since then, the race has always taken place during early December. It's become a civic event in Tucson.

Every year, my involvement with the Tucson Marathon follows a kind of arc. Right after the event there's a period of decompression. Then, for a while, the race is in the background and I think about other things. It starts to really gain momentum again in the fall—I need to race around getting permits and everything. By Thanksgiving, the Tucson Marathon is like an elephant in the

room: I don't want to keep thinking about it all the time, but it's
pretty much impossible to ignore.

• • • • •

I have so many memories from the marathons over the years,
especially the earliest ones.

Jackson was born in the summer of '95, and I remember with
some chagrin how a couple of years after that, Pat and I dragged
our 2-year-olds along with us to meetings with potential sponsors.
The kids would misbehave—well, behave like 2-year-olds. Disaster.
We were clueless about how inappropriate that was—really
oblivious. I can only imagine what must have been going on in the
minds of the professional people we were looking to for funding!
We were both such moms. It seemed normal at the time. After a
while, it began to dawn on me that as much as I *thought* it was okay,
it really was *not* okay.

Setting up for the marathon is always intense. Volunteers work
all night, and there's always at least one moment of panic. One year,
Elisa and a volunteer were handling the glamorous job of setting up
the portable toilets. They were positioning 25 of them out in the
desert, really in the middle of nowhere. Around four o'clock in the
morning, after drinking coffee all night, the volunteer ducked into
one of the potties. When he came out, he reported, "No paper," and
quickly entered the next one. Uh-oh. Same problem. After quickly
ducking in and out of the rest, he announced, "There's no paper in
any of them!"

Apparently, someone had stolen all the paper from every single
one. What would motivate someone to do something like that is
beyond me. Meanwhile, thousands of runners were about to start
arriving. Picturing the long potty lines typical at race events, Elisa
dug around in the truck and found, miraculously, a roll of paper

towels and two rolls of toilet paper. She had to stand there handing out individual sheets on a first-come, first-served basis.

Continuing with this theme, when Elisa lived in California, she had a friend named Sue Hunter who ran with her. Elisa, Sue, and some other women went on running trips together. Sue's husband was a biker—motorcycles, not bicycles—and he thought running was stupid. Finally, though, she got him to try it and, wouldn't you know it, Dave Hunter turned out to be a supercompetitive runner in his age group. Then Sue got burned out because Dave was better than she was and always pressured her to do more races. Funny how things turn out—but that's not the story.

What happened was that Dave and some of his running cronies came to do our marathon and one of the guys went to use the portable toilet. He came out with a bad look on his face. He'd somehow managed to drop his keys into the hole. Unfortunately, they weren't his house keys—someone could have helped him with that once he got back to California. They were the rental car's keys. There was nothing to do but reach in.

I think some kids must have too much time on their hands because they sure do like to cause problems for no good reason. One year we'd spent hours going from aid station to aid station setting up thousands of paper cups. You gotta figure that 4,000 runners times as many drinks as each one wants throughout a 13- or 26-mile course is a lot of cups. (Every year, we use 60,000 cups!) When we got back to the starting line, all the cups we'd set up a few hours before were knocked over and scattered everywhere—a huge mess. The little vandals! Tim had to make a quick trip across town to get more cups.

We learned our lessons from these incidents. Now we have backup cups and toilet paper. But there's no way of knowing what the next trick will be. It's all a matter of trying to be as well prepared as possible and staying calm no matter what.

Even in the face of roadkill. Coyotes love to play rather malicious tricks, and one was willing to die laughing. He died right in the middle of our course. Pay no attention to the dead coyote, folks! Just jump right over him! Once again, it was my son Tim to the rescue. He's the poor soul who ended up moving the carcass.

Probably our most embarrassing mistake happened at our first or second marathon. At the beginning of the race, Elisa was at the start for the half-marathon, I was at the start for the full marathon, and Pat was at the finish line. We were using the same clock for both races, so everything had to be completely synchronized. This involved calling each other, back and forth, to be sure we were together. Once the race got going, I started driving back down toward the finish, freaking out all the way, as usual. A point-to-point race is really complicated. Since you aren't finishing in the same place you start, a lot of stuff has to be shifted. It takes a lot of organizing and volunteers. Besides the logistics, I also worry about ADOT (the Arizona Department of Transportation) getting on our case for vehicles being parked along the road where they aren't supposed to be—I don't want our participants to get ticketed, and I worry, too, that someone could get hit. Believe me, when you're responsible for a marathon, there's plenty to worry about.

In any case, it was a rainy start, and I was just getting under way to the finish when Elisa's phone rang. It was Pat, and she was really, really excited. Runners were just finishing the half-marathon, and Pat couldn't believe what was happening: "We just had three finishers who have broken the world record on the half-marathon!"

Elisa was skeptical. My first thought was, "Wow, that would be some amazing publicity for our race!" After all, we *had* tried to create a fast downhill so runners would have a positive experience. A second later I realized that there was no way it could be true. Pat was so positive and so excited: "No, *really.* The timing company used two clocks!" I knew we had some good runners out there, but they were good by Tucson standards, not by world standards. It just didn't add up.

And it turned out that there was an explanation. As I wound my way down the hill, I came to a little turn-in road about a mile long. The course was designed so that runners turned in there, made a U-turn at the end of the road, and came back out. Because of the rain, a sheriff who was assisting with the race was directing runners past this road, having decided that it was too dangerous. I was livid! We had a certified course! How could this guy have taken it upon himself to redirect the race? Basically, he'd cut 2 miles off the half-marathon. There were no new world records that day.

Needless to say, this was a race director's nightmare. We tried to put it in the best possible light by saying that at least everyone had run the same distance. Also, thank goodness it was the half-, not the full marathon, that was affected. (We straightened out the confusion before those runners hit that part of the course.) So it did not affect anyone qualifying for Boston. We apologized to everyone, and a few refunds were given. Even now, some of our regular runners ask, "Is this going to be a short one or a full one?" Very funny.

• • • • •

These days, Elisa and I have a pretty good balance worked out. Most of the time she's behind the scenes making sure that everything is organized and together; she's a really good writer, so I'm always happy with our communications. I'm the front man, out there taking all the accolades—and, when things get screwed up, all the crap.

I really love the marathon, even though it is a ton of work. In coming years, I'm planning to hire a larger staff to take some of the pressure off of me. Every year, I'm amazed by the number of people and the infrastructure it takes—four different police departments, ambulances at the ready, printers and T-shirt people, and don't forget the portable toilets. We really, really need every one of our contributors to have a successful event. And they come through for us.

CHAPTER 12

CHUCK GILES

I have never had a trainer, a manager, or a coach. If I had, I might have done more as a runner, or done my races more efficiently. It's also possible that I might have done fewer events. I can recall numerous cases in which a friend or family member tried to discourage me from doing too many events in too short a time, strongly suggesting that I would do less well in any one of them if I took on too many. It's possible that if I had done fewer races, my results would have been better.

I do sometimes think about having someone more neutral than my husband (who has given me some great advice but also put a lot of the wrong kind of pressure on me) take over some of the strategic questions in my career: Which races should I run? How much rest should I take between events? When am I doing too much or too little? Tactically, a coach could help me decide when to speed up or slow down, when to keep going, and how to recognize when dropping out of a race is the best decision. For most of my career, I've been the one answering those questions.

I have received lots of encouragement from lots of people. One whom I should mention is Benny Linkhart, who was the first person to urge Jim and me to try ultrarunning. Benny is an amazing guy who has a really cool presence. He's 75 years old, and when he competed, he was always in the top 1 percent of his age group. Benny sort of "adopted" and mentored a number of runners in the Tucson area (mostly women, funnily enough), pushing them to do more with whatever talent they had. I was one of Benny's adoptees and trained with him for the 100-mile races by running the 17-mile loop of Bear Canyon. I recall that the first time we ran it, there was 2 inches of snow on everything—it was amazingly beautiful, a treat that's never happened since. Anyway, I really benefited from Benny's interest, but he wasn't truly my manager or coach.

Not until I met Chuck Giles in 2001 did anyone take a calculated interest in what I was really capable of or have a plan for helping me achieve my best. Chuck is an elite ultracyclist who has done some seriously amazing races and rides. He rode across Africa, from Cairo to Capetown; from the westernmost point of Australia to the easternmost point; and from Paris to Istanbul. He's crewed the approximately 3,000-mile Race Across America seven times—as well as winning once and placing third another time. He also—along with Craig Bellmann—won the Mojave Death Race (a discontinued event that earned its name) four times in a row.

When we met, Chuck was really excited about a particular ultra footrace. He had an idea of what it would take to win it and was looking for a protégé. When he heard about me from my best friend, Susy Bacal, whom I had met at the Tucson Racquet Club when I was pregnant with Andrew, he felt that I could be the one. Susy used to work as an attorney at Chuck's law firm, and he had mentioned this race to her when they were riding bikes. When he first broached the topic with me, I thought he was completely crazy.

Chuck is not really a runner, but athletics have always played a central role in his life. He's one of the smart athletes. Even though he played semipro baseball, he also got his degree and became a successful lawyer. I knew Chuck's reputation, so even though I was wary, I tried to keep an open mind.

The race in question was Badwater, that little 135-mile run across a burning desert and up the side of a mountain in the hottest month of the year. Right. Sign me up. Sure, I loved to run in the Sonoran Desert around Tucson, and yes, Jim and I had been doing some long races, and I'd done well in them. But I wasn't entirely out of my mind!

Later, I learned that Chuck had found out about the race while he was doing a long bike race organized by the same race director who puts on Badwater. Chuck had enlisted to help out as a race official a few times and was completely taken by how bizarrely extreme it was. Craig Bellmann does a very good imitation of what Chuck was like when he first got jazzed about the race: "They run in these *Lawrence of Arabia*-type outfits, and it's so hot, *their shoes melt!*"

It took Chuck a year to wear me down, but he kept working on me, refining his plan—not to mention his pitch—until, little by little, I began to sort of share his vision. Maybe I *could* do this race.

Since then, he has been in charge of my crew for four Badwaters, my 300-mile run in 2005, and other races. But to describe Chuck as my crew chief is selling him short. Chuck is the closest thing to a coach I've ever had.

At the world-class level, very few athletic events other than ultrarunning (and ultracycling) take place with no one watching. In my opinion, this is as much a part of the sport's uniqueness as the often extreme weather conditions, intense geography, and long distances involved. Spectators bring a certain energy to any competition and have a real effect on how an athlete performs. Try to imagine professional football or basketball teams competing in empty stadiums. Would they make the same plays if the stands were empty and there were no coaches? I doubt it. We'll never know, though, because just about the only elite athletes who perform in virtual solitude are ultrarunners. Many times I've been on a course with no one around for miles. Sometimes there have been other athletes in sight, but they have been competing against me, not cheering me on. Nor was there anyone checking out how the race was going and revising tactics accordingly, shouting encouragement or advice from the sidelines—well, Jim might be waiting at an aid station to yell, "Move it!" or "Get the lead out!"

That's changed since I met Chuck Giles.

In his work with me, Chuck is like a very good personal physician. He understands that the correct "prescription" in an ultra event involves not only the particular qualities and abilities of the athlete but also the time of day, year, and so on; the place; what happened yesterday; what's planned for tomorrow; and a dozen other factors.

Without a doubt, Chuck's own experiences as an elite ultracyclist have helped him arrive at this perspective. I bet that a lot of his ideas about how to direct and support me over the course of Badwater—from what and how much to eat to how to pace myself— were developed during some of the long bike races he competed in or crewed.

In his capacity as crew chief, I'd describe Chuck as authoritative but not authoritarian. He knows that committee decisions don't work in competitive situations when the clock is ticking, and he makes those decisions without screaming. I respect his understanding of the emotional and psychological elements of ultra events, as well as the physical requirements. Chuck understands because he's been there, even though I don't think everyone who's been there would necessarily understand.

For example, I'm not at all sure that I would be a good coach. As an athlete, I have certain capabilities—like being able to keep going despite pain, even though I do feel pain like everyone else. I don't know if I could work with athletes who don't have that capacity. I think to be a good coach you need to be able to really get inside somebody else's head—to perform a real act of creative imagination. I'm just not that creative. I think of myself as being very consistent, someone who—98 percent of the time—does her thing regardless of how she feels or where she is. It takes someone like Chuck to be able to read the signs, to know "what condition my condition is in" over the course of a race, and to address whatever issues need to be addressed.

One way in which Chuck really shines is as a problem solver. In fact, I believe that this is the real appeal for him of an ultra race like Badwater. He enjoys figuring out new and better ways of doing something. He loves to find the angle that hasn't been considered before. And then I'm the guinea pig for his genius. I say that jokingly because usually it's a good thing. At Badwater, a lot of Chuck's creativity has gone into coming up with innovative cooling systems. For instance, it was his idea to spray water on me from a bike. When bikes were banned from the race, he designed a spraying system built into a jogging stroller (also then banned). One of my favorite ideas was the slushy grape drinks made from semifrozen Ultra Fuel energy drink. Chuck had the idea of plugging a blender into the cigarette lighter of the crew van. They were an odd but wonderful luxury in that blast furnace in the middle of nowhere.

No matter how off-the-wall his latest invention might seem, it always has a practical side. And when it comes to rounding up a crew and keeping crew members organized over the course of a race that lasts more than 24 hours, he is all business and nothing but impressive.

Chuck had told Craig that he really wanted to crew for someone who had a chance at winning Badwater. When we met, that chance came for both us.

CHAPTER 13

SOME LIKE IT HOT:
BADWATER 1

I f you're ever stranded in the desert during the summertime, don't do *anything* during the day. If you can, find some shade and stay in it. If there's no shade and the sun hasn't come up yet, dig a hole and cover yourself with dirt.

This is the core message of every survival manual ever written. It's also the wisdom that has evolved in the snakes, lizards, spiders, box turtles, and assorted rodents who inhabit arid climates. They stay undercover, or under rocks, until the sun goes down.

Some of us don't have the sense that God gave animals. This is not the way the Badwater race is run.

In the middle of July, 80 runners, in groups of approximately 25, approach the starting line at staggered times between six o'clock and 10 o'clock in the morning. The less experienced runners start earliest and the "favorites" start later. (The logic is that the faster runners will pass the earlier starters, allowing the entire field to finish sooner.)

Regardless of when they take their first steps, everyone intends to run, walk, or crawl slightly more than 135 miles across the floor of Death Valley, a vast, barren salt flat; over steep mountain passes; and then into the town of Lone Pine, California, at an elevation of approximately 3,700 feet. From Lone Pine there is a further climb into the series of dramatic rock formations known as the Alabama Hills and then partway up the side of Mount Whitney to a height of more than 8,000 feet.

This race is an extremely unnatural thing to do. No animal in its right mind would undertake such a thing. That's the point, of course. Badwater is all about going against your instincts. Or rather, it's about continuing to run when you want to stop more than anything in the world.

Everyone who finishes Badwater in less than 60 hours wins a belt buckle. Sixty hours is actually quite a bit of time. You could almost walk the course and still get something to hold up your pants. But even walking the whole way wouldn't be easy; the longer you're out there, the more the elements take their toll—those who are exposed to the heat the longest frequently experience hallucinations. The winning times have generally been between 25 and 30 hours. Most people, of course, don't enter the event with the thought of winning. For many of the competitors, it's more of a trek than a footrace. They're happy and proud just to finish. And they deserve to be.

In this kind of environment, runner safety is naturally a major concern. Every participant is required to bring along a support crew to provide food, drinks, and first aid if necessary. A runner's crew typically includes four to eight people who travel in two vans so one can stay close by the runner if the other needs to go for supplies. Some crews are more spartan, having only two people in one vehicle. Being a crew member is very hard work. After the first 17 miles, which runners must complete without the assistance of a crew, crew members can accompany the runners for the rest of the race, and sometimes a crew member will run a significant portion of the race with the competitor.

There's a lot more to say about crews, and I'll get to it later on. They deserve a chapter of their own. First, I want to give you a picture of the Badwater terrain and all the agonies and ecstasies that certain runners—like me—actually choose to take on.

• • • • •

I love to race in the heat. I think that gives me a big advantage. I've always been addicted to saunas—the hotter the better. At home in Tucson, I'm used to running for 3 hours every day in temperatures of around 100 degrees. At Badwater it gets much hotter than that, which isn't really pleasant, but I'm able to take it better than most people, and it does eliminate a lot of the competition.

Once the temperature passes 100, it's amazing how much difference every degree makes. There's no comparison between 110 and 120. It's ridiculous. And when you approach 130, you're really on another planet.

One of my little eccentricities is not wearing sunscreen (except on my nose). Sunscreen gives me an intense feeling of claustrophobia. I feel like I'm suffocating, like my body can't breathe. Maybe sunscreen keeps your skin from burning, but you will definitely roast.

Until I did Badwater for the first time, I usually didn't do any reconnaissance on the courses I was going to run. That's changed as I've become more experienced as a runner. Now, before a marathon or an ultra event, I like to know where I'll be going. Being able to visualize the race beforehand helps me to prepare. At the time, however, Chuck had wanted me to check out Badwater in advance and I felt I would be better off not knowing what lay ahead. The most I would do was let Chuck take me to an overlook called Dante's View. He pointed down at this wasteland and said, "That's Badwater." It was like looking at the bottom of an ocean, but one that was completely dry. It was eerie to think that in a few hours I'd be racing down there.

The next day, we rose early and headed for the event. They say ignorance is bliss, but in this case it meant that all day and all night of the race, I would be surprised by each new horror as it arrived.

• • • • •

The year of my first Badwater, 2002, there were 79 runners—63 men and 16 women. Among our motley crew, my being a mom was not that unusual. It would have been pretty impossible to characterize this pack—doctors, lawyers, businesspeople, international racers, some ultra veterans, including Marshall Ulrich, who was planning on crossing Death Valley lugging a 200-pound rickshaw loaded with food and water; in other words, solo—no crew. Also running were Marine Corps Major Curt Maples, a guy in a bunny suit (who dropped out not very far from the start), and German ultrarunner Achim Heukemes, who was confidently predicting a win for himself.

I was running in the first flight, made up mostly of women. My hip had been bothering me the night before (one of many pains that come and go), so Craig, who I'd literally just met upon arrival in Las Vegas, had given me a massage. I was still slightly achy as I stood at the starting line. I hoped to be able to run it off.

Even at the start of the race, at 6:00 a.m., it was already 100 degrees. And it was unbelievably dry. One of the crews' major functions is to keep the runners as moist as possible, using spray guns or any means necessary. From miles 1 to 17, your crew is not allowed to pace you. So to cool me down, mine would drive ahead about a half mile, get out of the van, spray me down, and get back in and drive forward again. Other crews were driving much farther— maybe 2 miles ahead of their runners. So the runners were really parched by the time they caught up to their crews. After the first year of my crew cooling me more frequently (Chuck's inspiration), other crews got smart and copied us.

There were these white suits that you could buy that were supposed to reflect the sun, I think, or Pam said maybe they were for if there was a dirt storm. They weren't really sized for a smaller person. There was this headdress, like in *Lawrence of Arabia*. And these goggles— like old people wear when they have cataracts. Pam modeled it. She's so tiny. She looked like Marvin the Martian. And Craig had a heart attack—he didn't think she'd be able to breathe in it.

Pam ran in a T-shirt, jog bra, and shorts. Everyone said, "You're insane! You have to wear this suit or you'll die."

—Susy Bacal

For the runners in the lead, getting to Stove Pipe Wells, at around mile 40, at the far end of Death Valley, takes 6 to 8 hours. That means a full day of running through an otherworldly landscape of volcanic rocks, gravel, and glare. The pavement of the highway gets so hot that blisters are a major problem. The soles of your shoes can melt, so many runners go through several pairs during the race. The temperature on the floor of the valley varies slightly from year to year. During the 2002 race, the high was a very toasty 127 degrees.

Entering Towne Pass at mile 40 (the first of three passes in the race), the fierce wind was relentless, brutal, constantly buffeting, and completely drying. Running through this pass has been

described—very accurately—as like running into the blast from a
blow dryer. Towne is the first big elevation challenge. It's an uphill
of 18 miles. This comes late in the first day, after you've been out in
the heat since around sunrise. It's really, really hot. The road just
stretches on and on; you can't see the end of the climb for hours.

While I was being well cared for, the crew was fending for itself.
Craig had been trying since morning to find something edible for
himself. He only eats really healthy food, and I guess we hadn't packed
any of that—or at least nothing solid. He'd picked up a sandwich at
Stove Pipe Wells but didn't want to eat it—it was made of some kind
of pressed meat and had been in the hot van for a long time. Chuck
and Carol Trevey (a cycling friend of Chuck's who had both
completed and crewed the Furnace Creek 508-mile race) had taken
the other vehicle up ahead on their break and had a nice dinner—fish,
salad, and potatoes—at the Panamint Springs Resort at around mile
70. So Craig was hanging in there, half starving, waiting for his break
so he could finally get some real food. Finally it was his and Susy's
turn, and they headed for the restaurant. When they got there, the
place had just closed. My maternal instinct kicked in—I worried
about Craig being able to find something he could eat.

Meanwhile, my plan was to just keep going as steadily as possible.
I wasn't going to stop unless I had to throw up. I knew from the
general buzz as well as things that Chuck had told me that it was
normal for runners to stop for a few minutes for a massage or for
even longer to take a brief nap, just to get off their feet and try to
come up with some fresh energy. I was determined not to make
any stops. I did have to stop once when I felt a pain in my foot
right near the Panamint Springs Resort. It would have been nice
to stop there for a dip in the pool, but I just pulled off my shoe and
shook it. When no stone fell out, I realized that it was a huge blister
on my foot that was causing the pain. I didn't even want to see it. I
just put on my shoe and got going again. My foot hurt for a while

but then stopped, so I knew the blister had broken.

The heat was just stupid. Never mind the air temperature. The *road* gets up to 200 degrees. A lot of people run on the white lines, the theory being that the white reflects the sunlight and will be cooler. I ran in the dirt a lot, thinking *that* would be cooler. But I don't really think there *was* any "cooler."

I had a weird experience in the Panamint Valley. There's a pretty steep downhill for about 8 miles and then an uphill for about 4 miles to reach the resort. It was dark, and I had the impression that, rather than descending and rising, the road was flat the whole way. It was an odd illusion.

In spite of the hellacious conditions, my memories of the race are good ones. I just remember the awesome crew running or biking along with me, telling me stories to keep me entertained, spraying me down with water to keep me as cool as possible.

Another thing that's bizarre is that nothing stops for the race. The race goes through this terrain where everything else is happening as usual. During the day, new BMW models were being test-driven on the road we were running on. The guys on the crew were all into that. "Wow—did you see that car?"

I remember vividly at around mile 90, as we were approaching Pine Ridge—there is a 30-mile stretch that isn't demanding, just really long—Susy and Craig were practicing their Bon Scott imitations, singing AC/DC's "Highway to Hell" at the top of their lungs. It was really funny.

• • • • •

Badwater is unusual. It's the opposite of any other long run I've ever done. In most runs, during the day, you totally go for it and try to cover as many miles as you can. This is because at night—in the pitch-black, far from civilization—you have to run with a flashlight. It's awkward and slow. At Badwater, however, you're on a road. You don't need a flashlight to keep yourself on the path. Natural starlight in the dry, haze-free atmosphere does the job. The most intense moments visually are late at night. During daylight, you at least have a sense of where you are. The nighttime is surreal. The only things you see are the stars and moon and the small dome of light created by your crew and their vehicles. Outside that circle is blackness. Early on—from about mile 40—the runners spread out, so there's no sense of being part of a group event. You're really in your own little world.

After Panamint, the next big climb is Father Crowley, which tops out at mile 85. It's sickeningly steep, a 6 or 7 percent grade that just climbs and climbs. Like virtually everything else in this race, it goes on for a long time. Craig was cycling along with me. I don't know how he could even bike on a hill that steep. He'd switched on his little bicycle light. Finally, as we crested the hill, we came face-to-face with a full moon—it was so beautiful.

I was almost on automatic pilot, just following the van, ticking off the miles, not having much of an idea of where I was headed. From Father Crowley Point, I had the bike support and company of Scott Scheff, a triathlete from Boulder who makes ergonomic, "people friendly" products and had crewed the Race Across America several times with Chuck. Because I was in the first flight of runners to leave, it was hard for us to keep track of how we were doing relative to the course times of other runners who had gotten later starts.

Suddenly, at around two or three in the morning, the race director, Chris Kostman, drove up alongside us and gave my crew the amazing news that I was "comfortably" in the lead. The crew members all had walkie-talkies, so the news was quickly radioed to my pacer on the road.

Wow. Up until that point, I think we'd all been feeling like race "participants" who were trying to do well. And the race *had* been going well. Chuck had put together a good plan, and the crew was upbeat and supportive. We had not had any major problems. But even though I knew I had been running pretty consistently, this was beyond any of our expectations.

· · · · ·

Mile 90, for some reason, is called Darwin. I've never heard anyone mention why. There's nothing there; it's not a town or anything. Miles 90 to 122 are on a long downhill to Lone Pine in the Owens Valley. This is where the race is either won or lost. After this, you can still lose it by just dying, but there isn't another opportunity to make time. The irony is that nine times out of 10, by the time the runners reach Darwin, they're too tired to take advantage of the downhill. So maybe the name refers to Darwin's theory about the survival of the fittest.

As I closed in on Lone Pine, Susy was running with me. It was still very hot, at least 100 degrees. By this point in the race, most of the runners are actually walking. Cars whiz past on the highway— none of them have a clue about the colossal struggle being endured by the limping athletes on the shoulder of the road. At this point, if you let yourself think about it, you may feel foolish as well as exhausted. I was trying not to go there, concentrating instead on the mechanics: Am I getting enough to eat and drink? How comfortable is my "comfortable" lead? Could someone catch me?

· · · · ·

As we headed into Lone Pine, we passed a few motels, a pizza restaurant, a McDonald's, a gas station, a supermarket, and some supply stores for campers headed to Mount Whitney. Not that I was really paying attention to any of this, but at least it was something different than what I'd been looking at throughout the day before. Although it's not a desert like Death Valley, this area is also extremely dry. There is very little irrigation, because most of the water in the Owens Valley has been diverted to Los Angeles since early in the 20th century. This has kept towns like Lone Pine and Independence from the kind of overdevelopment that has overtaken communities on the other side of the mountain range. It also makes for a fairly bleak landscape.

In Lone Pine, there were actually some spectators. The race headquarters is usually in one of the motels there, and a few people cheer you on as you go by. And I do mean a *few* people. This all contributes to the surreal atmosphere of the race. It's true that Badwater is probably the best-known ultra event; it was even the subject of a feature article in *The New York Times*. As a rule, though, there aren't any *Times* writers on the sidewalks of Lone Pine. There might be a reporter from a nearby local paper. More people are likely to be filling their tanks at the gas station than watching the race.

At this point, the runners have covered about 122 miles, and the leaders have been on the course for 20 to 24 hours. The race is far from over, however. There's still the little matter of crossing the picturesque badlands of the Alabama Hills, and then the 8,000-foot climb up Mount Whitney.

To tourists watching the runners as they struggle through the town of Lone Pine, this must seem totally unbelievable. Most people who visit the area do so because of Mount Whitney, and they know how their cars and SUVs strain going up the steep mountain switchbacks. The idea that anyone who's already run across Death Valley would then run up the side of Mount Whitney is the craziest thing imaginable.

It was exciting to be in the lead going into Lone Pine. It was also deceptive and disorienting. There was still a long way to go in terms of the effort that would be required to ascend to Whitney Portal. It was 13 miles on the map. Thirteen miles is a half-marathon. It's a distance that runners are used to. You feel like you should automatically be able to do it, simply because you've gone that distance so many times before. Of course, you've never done it under these circumstances. And even in the best of circumstances, you can't really call it "nothing." If you are running a half-marathon, you might be able to do it in $1\frac{1}{2}$ to 2 hours. Here, minimally, you are looking at 3 to 4 hours. Thirteen miles, especially at this point, is *not* a piece of cake.

Despite the increased elevation, it was still over 100 degrees. As I rounded a bend with Susy, who would continue running with me until the end of the race, we finally got a look at the road going into the mountains. It shocked me. "You've got to be kidding," I said. "We're going up *there?*" The road is as steep as any mountain road in the world, switchbacking cruelly toward the finish. Above are stark, ragged vertical spires. The silhouette looks like the teeth in a shark's jaw. Just plain crazy. Here we go . . .

First there's a slow climb through the totally wild rock formations of the Alabama Hills. It was like the surface of the moon. Literally hundreds of Western films and TV shows have been shot here over the years. It is picturesque, but also really dead. Unlike in the Sonoran Desert around Tucson, there are no cacti, just rocks piled on top of each other. Then we came to the mountain itself, where the road gets much steeper, with one switchback following another. Running at any speed was impossible. I was walking. Walking slowly. Well, maybe staggering.

It was cruel. I knew I was near the finish, but I couldn't get a sense of how far it really was. At the very end, there were some distance markers: "3 miles," "2 miles." When you're only going about 2 miles an hour . . .

Finally, there it was: the tape across the road.

As you approach the finish line, the terrain abruptly changes from seemingly endless expanses of rocks and gravel to evergreens and pinecones. There are people around—some to cheer on the finishers, some to essentially "collect the body" of a friend or loved one who made it all the way there. And because it's the trailhead for climbing Mount Whitney, some people are there just for that and have no interest in the race. The tape at the finish line has to be pulled down repeatedly in order to let minivans pass.

As Susy and I were hauling ourselves into range, the crew was parking our vans. Then they rushed out to meet us and ran with us across the finish.

Crossing that tape was like dying and being born at the same time. I was literally crying, just letting out all the tension. Though I had managed not to focus on it, I had been scared throughout much of the race—it was so brutally hot, and I didn't know what was going to happen to my body. Now all I wanted was to sit down. There were a few folding lawn chairs and I just about fell into one of them. People were asking me all kinds of questions, and for once, Motormouth could barely get out two words.

I'd eaten hardly anything solid during the race (I later found out that I'd lost 6 pounds, in spite of drinking massive amounts of calories), so I was starving. We all went back to the hotel, where I had a bath—I couldn't even stand up to take a shower. Then I put on some clean clothes and went to dinner.

So we're going to go for dinner. Pam wanted, I don't know, a hamburger or steak—some large slab of beef.

But first, she peels off her shoes and socks. Her feet are just like hamburger—large blisters, blisters on blisters. Some are broken; you can see bloody flesh. And she pulls out this little kit—hydrogen peroxide, needles, gauze, ointment. She very casually pricks and drains all the blisters and cuts away all the loose skin, just like she's brushing her teeth. Just two of those blisters would have brought me to my knees. And she's acting like they're nothing. Then she puts her shoes back on and we go to dinner.

—Craig Bellmann

I barely slept that night. I was beyond bone tired, but my body was still crawling. I couldn't seem to convince it that the race was over.

The next day, Susy and I went for a nice little run and hike to see what we'd missed of Mount Whitney. I couldn't help thinking that long after I'd finished, eaten dinner, gone to bed, gotten up again, and enjoyed a morning run, people were still out there on the course, giving their guts to finish.

CHAPTER 14

MY CREW

There's a lot more to ultrarunning than just putting on a pair of running shoes and moving on down the road or trail. It took me a while to really appreciate that. I was already a fairly experienced ultrarunner before I understood the importance of having a band of helpers, otherwise known as a crew. At first, I just didn't see the need for them. I used to show up at 100-mile events with just Jim to help me. Sometimes we would be running together in the same event, so I never thought of Jim as someone who was there solely to support me. In fact, I didn't feel like I needed support. We'd leave some bottles of drinks and supplies in drop bags at a few aid stations, and that was that—fast and simple.

This was my choice, of course. I was aware that other people felt differently. Some wanted whatever help was allowed by the particular race. In many events, the runner is permitted to have a pacer, someone who runs beside him or her. In most ultra races, pacers are allowed for the second half of the race. Runners over 60 years old can have one the whole way. Pacers can have a powerful emotional effect. If everyone else has one and you don't, it can be demoralizing. Sometimes even I have felt a little deflated when it seems like everyone else has company and I'm running by myself.

On the other hand, a pacer may also be a psychological liability. Someone who starts out as a morale booster can turn into a heavy piece of baggage. If conditions are really bad and the pacer wants to quit, for example, a runner can get tired of helping the helper. During the Grand Teton 100 in 2005, conditions were so bad that pacers were dropping out, and a few runners dropped out with them. If I'd had a pacer in that event, I might have quit, too.

In general, I'd rather compete by myself if at all possible. I love to do training runs with another person, but races are a completely different experience. I like to get into a zone without having to worry about the person next to me. That's how I felt at the beginning of my career, and in most events I still feel that way.

When Chuck first started talking to me about Badwater, he said that I had to have a crew. In his mind, there was really no question about it. That's just the way it was. In the same way, he'd told me I needed to get my nutrition under control. He wasn't talking about my anorexia. I don't even think he knew about that. He was simply giving me instructions about what it would take for me to be competitive. And I think because he was telling me how to win, rather than how to not be sick, I was able to hear it—and *do* it.

But a crew? I already was aware of the kinds of extra emotional ups and downs that could be created by just one other person; having a crew sounded to me like it would compound that, that it would be like introducing another set of complicated and unnecessary relationships. And on one level, I felt that having a bunch of people servicing me was self-indulgent.

Of course, as with a number of other things, I was totally wrong about this and Chuck was right. Today, when I think about how I wanted to do the race without any support, it seems insane. At the time, I liked to think of myself as a self-sufficient running machine. Well, no one is self-sufficient at Badwater. It is literally impossible to complete the course without a really good support crew.

For most of even the longest races, a crew is not necessary. Aid stations work just fine. The difference between Badwater and other races is, if it needs to be said, the heat. You can't have aid stations there because the people manning the stations could not possibly sit out there exposed to the sun and heat all day—they'd all die of heatstroke. The only way to deal with Badwater's conditions is to keep wet, keep watered, and keep moving. You need a vehicle and a crew.

And it can't be just anybody. The crew has to be in good physical condition and well motivated. Crew members need to be selflessly dedicated to the runner's success. They also have to take care of their own needs during the race. If they don't, they'll fall apart before the runner does. After all, the crew is experiencing pretty much the same conditions as the runner. Instead of having a bunch of people seeing to their needs, however, they're the ones who are keeping it all together.

Attitude is really important. I think it's helpful if everyone has the ability to laugh. Otherwise, there could be a lot of tension. It also helps if you're able to stay awake for a long period of time, although crew members do spell one another for rests. I know that Susy, for one, normally likes to get at least 8 hours of sleep every night. When we do Badwater, she somehow always manages to stay awake the whole time.

With the innovations he brought to the event, Chuck increased both the importance of the crew and the difficulty of their task. By introducing the idea of continuously watering down a runner during the race, Chuck made it possible to run Badwater in times that were previously out of the question. For that to happen, there had to be crew members who could put his ideas into practice.

Chuck has been able to find, train, and motivate these people to do all the hard work that's required. I don't feel like it's an exaggeration to say that Chuck Giles "invented" Badwater as it's now run. He certainly invented me as a Badwater competitor, and that wouldn't have been possible without the crews that Chuck has put together.

> Number one, a crew will never win an event for a competitor, but a crew can lose the event. The competitor will fail if he or she isn't fed, watered, and cooled. Also, in a way, the crew members need to be amateur psychologists. They have to know when to kick the competitor in the butt. However, one thing you never do is deal with negative issues. You don't say anything that will make a runner fearful or upset. You never say, "You're not going fast enough," or "You're going too slow." You say, "It might be a good idea if you go a little faster."
>
> And it's also important to know when to disappear. It's good to have good talkers, people who can keep up a conversation. But sometimes Pam just wants to zone out. You need to be able to tell when that is.
>
> The single most important criterion for a crew member is to be willing to do whatever needs to be done to get the job done. One question I ask someone whom I'm considering for a crew is, "If Pam got diarrhea, would you be willing to wash out her shorts and get them back to her?" That's a litmus test! They really need to be willing to do anything.
>
> —*Chuck Giles*

I didn't understand the enormity of Chuck's contribution until I actually started running across Death Valley. It was six o'clock in the morning in July of 2002. Although the crew couldn't directly interact with me, I was allowed to have one support van with me for the first 17 miles. Susy and Craig were in the van. They could only drive along the course with me and then park by the side of the road and wait for me to catch up. They couldn't run with me. At mile 17 there was a switch—Chuck joined me on his bike and Carol Trevey took the wheel of the van, manning the flow of bottles of fluids.

During the first stages of the race, the crew needs to be in very close touch with the runner. This was especially true in 2002, when the weather was unusual even for Death Valley. The heat was absolutely amazing. Before long, it was approaching 130 degrees. Chuck rode beside me on that bike for 15 miles, spraying me with water the whole time. Cycling was probably even more difficult than running, but Chuck was totally committed to the effort. Having an energy force like that beside me was like being plugged into a nuclear power plant. There was just no way to be anything but positive and upbeat, even in conditions that ordinarily would be intolerable.

Of course, there was more to come. The first 40 miles of Badwater are a gradual uphill. Then there's a very steep climb between miles 40 and 60—a 5,000-foot ascent with the hot wind blowing in your face. All I could do was look up at the mountaintop in front of me and wonder if I'd ever get there. When Chuck's shift ended, Craig took over and pedaled the bike up that climb, cooling me down with the spray bottle the whole time. Very few people could ride a bicycle even on level ground in that kind of heat. This was an 8 percent grade, against the wind.

In addition to his spraying skills, I really relied on Craig to keep me distracted, or just entertained. As he biked along, he told me stories about his family and his travels and just nutty stuff. Once he told me a story about a trip he and a friend had taken to Mexico.

They were looking for a famous shaman or something—someone the Beatles had apparently visited or talked about. As it happened, this woman had died, but they heard that her daughter was still living. So they ended up taking a bus into rural Mexico. There were chickens on the bus—everything was very primitive. They found a guide who spoke some of the Aztec dialect, and because Craig spoke a little Spanish, they somehow managed to communicate just enough. Craig still hadn't been sure if they were going to the right place or if they'd ever get back... I'm not sure that I remember Craig's stories right, but certain pictures stick in my head—and some of them are pretty strange.

I've traveled quite a bit, so I can always think of a story to tell Pam to keep her mind off the miles. This one story I was telling her was about going to see a famous *curandera* [healer], who, it eventually turned out, had died. We found out that her daughter was still living way back in the jungle, very remote. So we had to get a guide. I'm used to taking this kind of trip—going into remote places, trying to get out alive, hiking, river rafting. I have an expression for *remote*: "500 miles from the nearest witch doctor." Anyway, we found the daughter, Maria, and she invited us in. And there was a guy lying on the bed who was dead. Clearly the medicine hadn't worked. Maria gestured for us to sit down next to the dead guy. This was just normal in their world. They're more comfortable with life and death.

Anyway, this is the kind of thing I'd talk about, and sometimes Pam would ask a question or sometimes just acknowledge something with a smile or a nod.

—*Craig Bellmann*

At mile 60, there's a steep downhill, and then there's another climb between miles 75 and 90. It's easy to get disoriented after going up, down, and then up again. It's also easy to get depressed, which is what happens to a lot of runners. To keep the energy flowing, it's important to have fresh crew members at all times. Fatigue is contagious. It's difficult enough if the runner gets tired. If a tired runner is surrounded by a tired crew, that is not good. Chuck does a great job of keeping my crew fresh. As I've said before, he is the boss. I have this memory of Craig being in the middle of one of his stories when Chuck told him it was time to let someone else pace me. Craig wanted to finish the story so I think, in effect, he told Chuck to wait a minute. That didn't go over so well. My memory is of a brief, well, not exactly power struggle, but a brief heated disagreement. I mentioned this to Craig once. He doesn't remember it as any major blowout. Considering that I can't remember who won the argument, it's possible that I was just a little out of it and "hallucinated" that.

· · · · ·

Even after hearing stories—even after reading this book—I don't think anyone who has never run Badwater can truly understand how demanding the experience is—how long, how slow, and how incredibly hot. I've heard that at least 40 people from various crews have, at one time or another, collapsed on the course and needed IV fluids. During one of her shifts in our first Badwater, Susy had run only a mile or two with me when she ended up overheating. She paid so much attention to taking care of me that she forgot to take care of herself. That was an anomaly for our crews. Usually Chuck is great about preventing that.

Susy totally gave it up for me at that event. She literally gave me the shirt off her back! By the time we got to Lone Pine, it was

6:00 a.m. and I was getting cold. I'd been running in a sports bra
with no shirt. Chuck rummaged through the van but couldn't find
anything else for me to wear, so he told Susy to give me her shirt. It
smelled like Susy and a combination of all the day-old scents in the
van. I liked the aroma, but I don't think I was very coherent at that
point. I just said, "It smells." I meant it in a good way!

* * * * *

Since Chuck revolutionized Badwater with his crewing innovations,
the race has become much more competitive. At first I was criticized
for having such a hands-on crew. Then other runners immediately
copied Chuck's methods. Everyone started using bicycles and spray
bottles—until bikes were banned in 2005.

That was only part of the change. Now everyone uses the
whole concept of having a crew that is totally involved with the
runner throughout the race. It's difficult to find individuals who
can make this commitment. In addition to the physical effort,
there's the expense involved—people have to miss work in the
middle of the week. Crewing for Badwater is not something to
take lightly.

For a crew to work really well together, everyone should know
each other, but not too well. If people are too close, the experience
can get pretty claustrophobic. And, too, when people know each
other too well they give themselves permission to whine. I definitely
have been guilty of that myself. That's why having my husband as
part of my crew would not work!

To put it really simply, a crew is something like another family.
It's also like the staff at a business, or maybe even a military unit.
The authority of the crew chief is strong and unquestioned, which
is not the way things are in most of the families I've seen lately. For
me, being part of a group like that is very reassuring. Knowing that

these people will be with me until the end of the line is a really
secure feeling.

At Badwater, every competitor walks the last few miles. It's
almost impossible not to. Then there's a bend in the road about 100
yards before the finish. That's where runners and their crews always
manage to break into at least a trot and cross the line together. I
always try to show my appreciation at that point, to say thank you.
It's not easy when I'm really worn out.

Even if I can't always show it, the way I feel is proof of what my
Badwater crew means to me. It's not that I wish the race would go
on longer (no one could possibly say that!), but I do wish that
another one would start right away, with the same crew. I can only
hope that they feel the same way.

CHAPTER 15

BADWATER TOO

A s the overall winner of Badwater 2002, I didn't see a reason to do the event again the following year. Everything had come together so well for my first try. It had been an almost perfect race. There was no good reason to do it again, except to improve on my time. Maybe I'm not the wisest person when it comes to making these decisions. I did think I might be able to go faster.

I was also aware that some people in the running community perceived my 2002 win as a fluke. Supposedly I had done well only because I had started the race at six o'clock in the morning. Never mind that all the female runners had started at six—maybe somehow this had given me an advantage. It was annoying. To work really hard for something and then be told you didn't deserve it— that's a great motivator. I also loved what at least one person said: that a woman winning Badwater was so suspect that maybe they needed to do some chromosome testing on me. Well, I'd already given birth to all three of my sons by then, so any kind of testing they wanted to do would have been redundant!

In any case, I spoke to Chuck about running Badwater again. I'm sure Chuck realized that there was a possibility things might not go well the second time. He also knew there was a chance I would do even better. So we agreed to enter again, with Chuck as my crew chief once more.

Craig couldn't make it that year. Susy was with us again, and Benny Linkhart joined us, too. It was great to have him with us—by then I'd known Benny for almost 15 years. It couldn't have been easy for a man his age to be part of a Badwater crew, but he offered to step in. Also on the crew was Lee Moore, a flight attendant who had crewed three Races Across America with Chuck and also had officiated Badwater before I started doing it.

I knew that I would have to deal with more pressure than I had the first time. I was aware of the controversy about whether a woman could win twice. The media coverage was more intense, and there were a lot of good runners, including one of Brazil's top ultrarunners. I definitely felt the pressure; I felt like others were setting my goals for me. This was predictable, maybe, but I still didn't like it.

The night before the race, Jim said, "Dean Karnazes is going to run."

I said, "Who's Dean Karnazes?"

I really didn't know. Jim seemed surprised that I hadn't heard of him. "He's a really great runner. He's done the Western States 100-miler a bunch of times and some other long races."

"Well . . . great."

This time there was going to be a 10 o'clock start. Many of the runners were wearing that same peculiar clothing I'd first seen the year before: the loose-fitting, light-reflecting white outfit that looks like a biohazard suit. When all the runners were waiting at the starting line, someone said, "There's Dean Karnazes." I looked and saw that he was wearing one of the heat suits. It's not an outfit that makes a very flattering first impression. But it was already pretty hot at that point, so maybe the suit was helping.

Because of the later start, the early stages of the race were hotter than I'd experienced the previous year—about 30 degrees hotter. Instead of wearing the white suit, one of my secret weapons was something that Benny introduced: a women's knee-high stocking filled with ice and knotted at the open end. Draped over the back of my neck, it worked wonders. But Badwater was *still* hot.

Chuck said, "Yeah, it's hot. But once the climbing starts, things'll cool off because of the altitude." That's what makes Chuck such a great crew chief. Without sounding insincere, he always manages to put a positive spin on things. As far as he's concerned, the glass is always half full. That has a hugely beneficial effect when you're in a physically stressful situation. There have been several times during my Badwater races when an encouraging remark has been a really big help. And encouragement was more than welcome. This year I knew what lay ahead of me and how tough it would be. Despite that, I can't say that I had a different overall strategy. My plan, like before, was just to keep running without making any stops.

In the first stages of the race some runners were ahead of me. Then I started passing one after another. Pretty soon, I thought I was in the lead. My crew, however, informed me that I was actually in third place, behind a German runner and Chris Bergland, who worked for Kiehl's, a personal-care-products company and corporate sponsor of the event. I didn't know anything about Chris. Chuck told me he was an ultra triathlete who possibly had never run much farther than the 72 miles of his signature race. It was likely that he had little experience with distances or conditions like Badwater's. Chuck guessed that Chris would eventually fold. Meanwhile, I passed the German runner.

Chris was still an hour ahead as I made my way across the

Panamint Valley after the first climb. As I started up the second big climb of the race, someone told me that Dean Karnazes was in third place and gaining on me. At this point, I wasn't feeling very well. Honestly, I felt like I was falling apart. I was determined to finish the race. Beyond that, it seemed like the best I could hope for would be third place. I figured Dean would pass me and either he or Chris would win.

Just as I was having these thoughts, Benny came up with the kind of encouraging statement that I'd heard so often from Chuck. He said that he was really proud of me just for competing, and that it would be a great accomplishment if I finished the race. I had actually slowed to a walk at that point, but Benny's words energized me.

So I started running again. Pretty soon I heard that Dean was now having a hard time. As is usual when I hear that about a competitor, I got even more energy. Maybe I could get second place after all. Of course, second was not what I'd had in mind when I entered the race.

I kept running through the night, and at around dawn the next morning—at around mile 100—I learned that Chris was now only 5 minutes ahead of me. I caught up with him a short time later, and he turned out to be a real class act. He shook my hand as I passed him. It was a gracious gesture. It was also a little shocking because, even for these extreme circumstances, his hand was abnormally hot. I thought he needed to get some help. His crew seemed to be inexperienced, which may have had something to do with the trouble that Chris appeared to be having. I had to keep going, but I asked my own crew to do what they could to get him cooled down.

It's hard to describe what a moment like that is like, in the middle of such an intense event. It's all kind of surreal. I was calling Jim on a cell phone to tell him I was in the lead. Just then Chris Kostman, the race director, pulled up on his motorcycle with the news that

Dean had recovered. In fact, he was now only about 30 minutes behind.

I was coming to the final climb, 8,000 feet up Mount Whitney. At the end of a race like that, you already feel like you've given everything that you have. It's hard to find the incentive to give more. Susy, who knows me very well, hit upon the perfect motivator: She promised that she would give me one massage for every minute I could cut off the time it took me to go up the mountain the previous year.

When the Mount Whitney climb begins, the crew likes to take turns walking with me. It really is mostly walking—or maybe power hiking—but rarely running. Benny was with me, and I was venting my anxiety. I asked him, "Honestly, what do you think my chances are of winning this race?"

Benny said, "I won't kid you, Pam. Your chances are 20 to 1."

With Susy's promised massages in mind and Benny's odds ringing in my ears, I threw my back into it and managed to save 20 minutes. Those minutes were critical. I wound up beating Dean Karnazes by only 25 minutes.

And then I threw up.

I did not beat my own 2002 time. I was about a half hour slower than the year before, and it was a very hard race. But it was exciting, too. It was a new experience for me to feel pressure like that instead of just showing up and running in any way I felt like. Now other Badwater runners were starting to focus on me.

They weren't the only ones, either.

CHAPTER 16

THE MAN
FROM IPANEMA

A friend who's a history buff told me something interesting about the Olympic Games. When the Games began in ancient Greece, footraces were the main events, but women were not allowed to participate. Women weren't even allowed to watch. Every 4 years, the games attracted thousands of spectators, all of them male. This went on for almost a thousand years. At one point, a separate set of games was established "for girls only." Men were allowed to watch those, of course. And the women's competitions never became as important as the men's.

We like to think that today things are different, but it wasn't until 1967 that Kathrine Switzer became the first woman to enter the Boston Marathon, by registering as K. V. Switzer. When the race director discovered she was a woman, he tried to throw her out. Women weren't officially permitted to run Boston until 1972. And only since 1984 have women been allowed to compete in the

Olympic marathon. In my own experiences, I've noticed that there's still something about a woman doing well in sports that makes some men uncomfortable. What makes them even more uncomfortable is the possibility of a woman beating them.

In the 2002 Badwater race, I was the overall winner. I also set a new course record of 27 hours, 56 minutes—so far, so good. In the following year's race, I encountered another athlete who seemed to radiate a lot of the tensions of male-female competition. He was a Brazilian ultrarunner, apparently one of the best in his country. He looked as if he'd just stepped off the beach at Ipanema. He had the sleek, muscular body of a surfer or diver and was covered with a thin film of oil that gave him an iridescent sheen. Bright orange running shoes completed the look.

Before the race, I felt that the Brazilian runner was very focused on me. He got off to an extremely fast start. But he also came to an extremely fast stop. Around mile 30 he and I were literally side by side. In a race like Badwater, where runners get very spread out— with *miles* between them—this was weird. I was keeping to my own pace, running on the white line at the side of the road, and he stayed glued to me, running right beside me. My crew's bike could not even get between us in order to spray me down. This went on for 5 miles. Really ridiculous. Finally I realized the only way to get rid of this guy was to speed up a bit, even though I didn't want to do that at this point in the race. When I did quicken my pace, he fell away. I later learned that he actually left the course (which is permitted) and laid down for 4 or 5 hours. Did he have a problem with a woman passing him? It's ironic to describe someone as having frozen up in the heat of Death Valley, but that's exactly what seemed to happen. Although he later returned and completed the course, he'd lost a huge amount of time.

The Brazilian's reaction was definitely extreme. But he wasn't the only one who might have been loath to lose to a woman. The year after that, the guys got serious about beating me—or so I heard. There were all these rumors about how they were training—for the race in general, yes, but the subtext was that they were going to take out Pam Reed. Except for the added pressure, I found this funny— even flattering.

Come to think of it, a woman winning at Badwater was probably a very good thing for that race. It got the race a lot more attention than it had had before. Chris Kostman said that the third year I ran, after two wins, the field was the deepest they'd ever had. I'll bet some of those runners underestimated the difficulty of the race. They probably thought, "Man, if a *girl* can win it, it can't be *that* tough."

Granted, not all men have issues with women athletes. And you could say that it's more about not wanting to lose to *any* competitor than it is about not wanting to let a woman best them. But it can't be denied that many male athletes become a special kind of crazy when they think they might lose to a woman. From childhood, it's ingrained in all of us that guys are stronger, tougher, faster. This stereotype is so strong that it takes constant struggle to break through it, even in my own family.

When Jim and I first met, it was he who encouraged me to enter triathlons and ultra events. Jim could see that I was really good, and he was proud of and encouraged me, which made me very happy. I really wanted that recognition. At the beginning, Jim may have thought that with all his encouragement I could be almost as good as he was. When I started to excel beyond his expectations, I think that wasn't all that great for him. And in a marriage, what isn't great for one spouse is probably going to be stressful for the other.

My husband is a really talented athlete and a very competitive person. He's always enjoyed doing marathons and triathlons, and he's good! But the way things have developed, sometimes he's felt a sense of competition with me—not just about winning or losing but also, given that we are married, about the time and effort I devote to my sport compared to what he's able to commit. As I've become more and more devoted to running, Jim has given more and more to his work—partly to finance my running. During the tax season, weeks go by when he seems to be constantly at his office. And for my part, even though I take care of the house and the kids, I know it sometimes must seem as if I'm constantly "on the road," whether it's running 20 miles a day at home or traveling to an event in who-knows-where. So there is tension about who "gets to be the athlete" that I don't think would be as prominent in a family in which it's the guy who does the running.

I think a lot about how lucky I am, with our society being the way it is, to have a partner who is willing—even if he sometimes complains—to support me as I pursue my sport. I'd like to think that male athletes who have families also recognize that someone is giving up a lot to enable them to train and compete.

CHAPTER 17

RUNNING THE WORLD,
A DAY OR TWO
AT A TIME

When I won Badwater the first time, in 2002, there was a lot of buzz about how my win might have been a fluke. It didn't feel like a fluke to me—I had gone the full distance, like any other finisher. But what did I know? Did I have an advantage because I began in the first flight of runners? Was my crew's exceptional care *too* good? *Was* it a fluke?

Chuck didn't think so. He encouraged me to go back the following year to clear up any doubt. So that, as I've recounted, is what we did.

After I won my second Badwater, Roy Pirrung, captain of the U.S. team for the World 24-Hour Run, an international 24-hour race, contacted me. Roy wanted to know if I'd be interested in joining the team that would compete that fall in the Netherlands, in a small town called Uden, relatively near Amsterdam. Usually you had to run a qualifying race to be included. Because I had won overall at Badwater twice, Roy said they'd waive that requirement.

The invitation was extended in July 2003; the event was to be held in October. I was excited and very honored about being asked to participate, and I was really happy that Jim wanted to go with me. When you do a run like that, you need someone to help you out, keep your stuff together, get you things you need, and so forth. So to have him along would be great. We were both excited about the trip. My ticket was paid for, but we had to buy one for Jim. This was not a puddle jump to a nearby Western state—it cost four times what we usually paid for one of those trips. Yes, winning Badwater upped the ante in more ways than one. My life in running was becoming ridiculously expensive.

The very day we were supposed to leave, Jim decided not to go. When we'd made our plans in July, it had not occurred to either of us that October is an extremely busy time in the accounting business. October 15 is almost as big for taxes as April 15, and Jim just didn't feel he could leave. This completely derailed me. I was scared. I'd been to Europe before, but never on my own. I didn't want to go alone. I didn't know what the experience would be like, and I wouldn't have anyone to lean on.

Nevertheless, I managed to get out the door and onto the plane. At the race, I was really reliant on the other runners' helpers. People were willing to help me out, and once I quit worrying, things were fine. I found my pace and locked into it. A lot of people mentioned that they were impressed by how steady I was. I think this is a hallmark of my running style.

It was a beautiful day, and with 11 countries taking part, it turned out to be quite an exciting race. The American women did really well overall, placing fourth as a team among the women. But the real drama was with the guys. Right at the finish, Ryoichi Sekiya of Japan and Paul Beckers of Belgium were neck and neck. Beckers finally prevailed, logging 167.8 miles. The top man for the United States was John Geesler, who placed 11th among all the men, with 148.7 miles. I took first place among the U.S. women and sixth among all women, with 134.86 miles. Irina Reutovich of Russia was first with an amazing 147.3 miles.

After that, I got a lot of invitations to travel and run. Unfortunately, that was the first and last time my airfare was paid for.

Next I was invited to compete in the 2003 U.S. 24-hour race, the San Diego One-Day Race, taking place just 3 weeks later, on November 8. The international race had given me confidence in my ability on a level track, so the decision to go to San Diego was not a difficult one. I ended up breaking the American women's record by running 138.96 miles.

Unless you are very well-trained—and I wasn't—numbers have tremendous power. Once I knew I'd hit the record, that knowing went straight to my body. I immediately slowed down. Jim, who was with me, kept saying, "Pick it up! You're going to be so mad at yourself later! You'll never know how much better you could have done." He was right, of course. But once you've broken a record, it is very hard to go on and smash it. Doing that takes tremendous mental power.

· · · · ·

The following year, I received another invitation, this time to compete as an individual in Surgères, France, at the international 48-Hour Track Championship race. In spite of some mishaps, this turned out to be a great trip since Jim and the boys all came along.

My guys had listened time and again to the audiobook version of Jon Krakauer's *Eiger Dreams: Ventures Among Men and Mountains*. I think they probably could recite it from memory. Krakauer talks about hanging out with all the climbers in Chamonix. I had the impression that Chamonix was the Jackson Hole of France, only with bigger mountains. That was our first destination, and it was gorgeous. The mountains—Mont Blanc and the nearby Swiss Matterhorn—are incredible.

There were a couple of bummers on our trip, one that happened one day when I took over the driving. We decided to drive through the 6-mile tunnel through Mont Blanc that leads from France to Italy. Partway through, Tim said, "Did you see that light?" I had, but I didn't know what it was. I continued driving through the tunnel, finally popping out into Italy. There I found out what the light had been: a speed trap. The police pulled us over and wanted us to pay something like $600 on the spot. I was going maybe 15 miles over the limit. I hadn't noticed that I was going that fast (about 50 kilometers per hour), and my speed had seemed safe compared to that of the other drivers in the spacious tunnel. Either the Italians, who are notorious for their bad driving, take speeding more seriously than you would think or the whole thing was a scam. After a discussion, the cops settled for $350. On top of that, we realized we'd all left our passports in France. Though that was only 6 miles back, it was still a different country. So we couldn't enter Italy after all. That ended that.

A few days later, we had another costly incident while traveling by train across France to its west coast. All throughout France we'd heard warnings to watch our belongings, so I had been keeping a close eye on my stuff. At Bordeaux I must have let down my guard. A guy bumped into me as he was climbing on board the train. A while later I realized that he'd somehow managed to get my wallet. I had just gotten a fresh supply of euros—not to mention the credit cards that were in there. It was not fun.

When we got to Surgères, all fun and games stopped. It was time for everyone to get to work. It was really cool to have a four-man crew—all of them family—taking care of me. Jim is the best at keeping all the details straight, and he got everyone organized into shifts.

The accommodations in Surgères were unique. Each of the 30 runners had a little trailer with his or her name on it. My family had also taken a hotel room only about 50 yards from the course, making everything pretty convenient and as comfortable as you can be when you're running for 48 hours straight. Adding to the unusualness of the experience was that this race is part of some kind of a celebration. The dirt track runs for less than a quarter mile around a fenced-in area, within which there are lots of parties going on. People were eating, drinking, cooking hot dogs—make that *saucisson*—and everyone was smoking. For one section of the loop about 25 yards long, someone can run beside you to pace you. I got a kick out of Jackson hooking up with me there every time I went around. Meanwhile, lots of French people were having the time of their lives, partying, occasionally leaning over the fence between us to yell, "Go Pah-mah-lah!" through gusts of cigarette smoke. It was very strange, but fun.

With my four guys spelling each other, I hope it wasn't as boring for the kids as it could have been. (Even a party can get old when it goes on for too long.) There was one point when I truly felt I could not keep going. All the runners there were the best in the world. I was feeling a little overwhelmed by the caliber of the other runners and wondered what *I* was doing there. Fortunately, Andrew's calm advice to just keep going was the gentle kick in the butt I needed. When it was all over, at 4:00 p.m. on Sunday, I placed second among the women, after Edit Berces of Hungary; finished fourth overall; and broke the U.S. age-group record with a run of 212 miles.

Then we headed to Paris for some more sightseeing. Because the weather was rainy and generally rotten, we were able to get tickets to the French Open without any trouble. Watching Roger Federer, a Swiss player who has won the U.S. and Australian Opens two times each and Wimbledon three times, was a highlight for Tim.

• • • • •

My second World 24-Hour Run was in the Czech Republic in November 2004. Jim went with me, and we were excited about getting to see what seemed like a "new" country, since it was no longer part of the Soviet Union. Of course it wasn't new at all—in Prague everything seemed incredibly old. It did not have the war-torn look of some other places we saw and it was clean, but nothing appeared to have been refurbished in a long time, and there was little that resembled a contemporary city. Also—not that we should have expected them to—nobody spoke English. And our Czech was not so good, either.

Getting something to eat was an adventure. I kept trying to ask for salad and getting things that I couldn't quite identify. Meat seemed plentiful (which was great for Jim), as did some sort of stew or goulash. And beer was both abundant and cheap, costing about the equivalent of 50 cents. We were traveling with some athletes who did not drink any alcohol, and they were a little shocked to discover that while you could get a beer for a half-dollar, a soda was about $3.

Brno, where the race was to be held, fulfilled every American stereotype of a Soviet city—pretty grim. All the buildings looked pretty much the same, making it very hard to differentiate what was what. When we finally found a grocery, it seemed to be stocked with nothing but Coca-Cola, Fanta (the Czechs seem to love this soda), chocolate, and maybe six loaves of bread. We rarely realize just how spoiled we are in the United States. This trip made that clear.

Ironically, we American runners were nonetheless a motley-looking crew. In Uden we had looked like a team, sporting matching singlets and shorts in red, white, and blue. Now, whatever funding that had existed apparently had dried up. Unlike the Japanese, the French, the Finns, the Swedes, the Germans, and the competitors from other rich countries, all of whom had matching uniforms of some kind, we were every man and woman for him- or herself. I used the opportunity to flash my Tucson Marathon tee. Still, I admit that I would have preferred to have the cohesiveness of some kind of uniform uniting us.

The course was outdoors, on sidewalks that wound all over—lots of twists and turns, up a small hill, past what looked like housing projects, past a parking lot. It was a bit on the crazy side. And wouldn't you know it, it rained.

The most surprising thing for me was that in the parking lot there was a big movie screen like you would see at a drive-in movie theater. But there weren't any cars—just people standing in the parking lot watching the movie. The dialogue was in Czech (I assume), but the music was American. And there those people stood—in the rain. Approximately every 12 minutes, as I made the loop, I'd catch a short bit of the film.

I came in sixth among the women, and our American team placed third.

After the race, Jim and I went to Vienna for a day before flying home. On the last morning of our trip, I got up early, as is my habit, and went for a run. With few exceptions, all cities feel the same to me, especially when it's not yet daylight. It doesn't matter whether they are in the United States or elsewhere, they're all buildings and sidewalks. New York has the green expanse of Central Park; I've really enjoyed running in Hyde Park in London; Chicago has some great running space along Lake Michigan. And to be fair, I know that a lot of other cities have great places to run also. But usually when I'm staying in a hotel, I don't find myself near those features.

On this particular morning, my experience was much the same: buildings and sidewalks, no surprises. Until I saw . . . something. Through the hazy darkness shone a huge circle of lights. I had no idea what it was. All I could think was, "Is that a UFO?" I'd never expected to see one, but what else could it be? I ran back to the hotel to tell Jim.

By the time we got back to where I had seen my UFO, day was breaking. Now I could clearly see . . . a Ferris wheel. Oh.

• • • • •

In 2005, I'd done the 300-mile race, which I'll talk more about a little later, then the triple marathon (the London Marathon, then the Boston Marathon backward and forward) before heading off to France to do the 48-Hour Track Championship again. This really should have been a clear lesson to me on when to say no. I was doing too much. My body just did not want to be at the race in France.

Over the course of that race, I had to stop for a massage seven times. At one point, Irina Reutovich confided to me that she was having a lot of pain, too. She said she was having liver problems and showed me a weird contraption that looked like a dog brush with individual metal spines embedded in a flexible rubber base, but with pins rather than semiblunt spines. She tucked it into her clothing— behind her neck, held by the cross strap of her sports bra, or against her abdomen, held in place by her shorts. It was some kind of self-acupuncture that she claimed was very effective. Wild.

In any case, it wasn't my race. I ran only 182 miles. Among the women, the day belonged to Irina Koval of Russia. She had started the race like a bat out of hell and somehow had managed to sustain that. I placed sixth among the women and something like 12th or 14th overall. I wasn't the only one who had crashed and burned, however. My fellow detonators included my countryman John Geesler and Japan's Ryoichi Sekiya, the world record holder in the event.

• • • • •

Also in 2005, I was again invited to compete with the U.S. team in the international 24-hour race, this time in Austria. Unfortunately, the race was being held only 3 days after Badwater. Even I am not crazy enough to try to do those events back-to-back. I stayed home that year and had another run at Death Valley. More on this later!

The following February, I was invited to run the 48-hour race again, this time in Taipei, Taiwan, on a pay-your-own-way basis. I was very grateful to have sponsors Red Bull, PowerSox, and Mike Kasser's Holualoa real estate firm helping me out. Red Bull helped fuel the run, and I switched back and forth between my Holualoa Tucson Marathon T-shirt and my PowerSox hat and tee.

I'm sorry to say that this turned out to be my weakest effort in this event by far. I ended up 18th woman, with an unremarkable distance of 121.5 miles. Smile! But I learned a valuable lesson.

With races at high altitudes, there's a lot of debate among runners about how far in advance you should arrive in order to acclimate. For people from lower altitudes, 2 weeks seems to be ideal—though if you have a life outside of running, it's also unrealistic. A similar question arises when jet lag may be a factor. In the case of Taiwan, I think I misgauged it. I arrived 3 days before the race—just far enough in advance for my body to begin to realize it was on another clock. If I had it to do over again, I think I'd just show up the day before the race and run it before my body got a clue.

●　●　●　●　●

I'm really lucky that as a result of my running I've had the opportunity to travel—and, when we could afford it, to take my family with me. After my kids got too big to fit in the jogging stroller, there was a long period of time when they were not that involved with my running. As they've gotten older and my career has taken us to some interesting destinations, I think these trips have opened up their world a bit.

CHAPTER 18

RUNNERS I ADMIRE

I'm not a very good spectator. For me, it's just much more natural to be doing rather than watching sports. And while I appreciate great athletes, it sometimes takes me a while to wake up to someone's talent, especially if that person has gotten lots of publicity. I know that's weird. I just have an inverse reaction to any kind of hype.

Michael Jordan is a really good example of this. There was a period in the 1990s when, if you listened to all the publicity, it seemed like he was the king of the world. Immediately, my reaction was that this must be mostly hype. How could anybody be that good? Of course, when I watched him, I could see that he really was a great competitor. Apart from his physical skills, he seemed to have an incredible will to win that affected not only his own team but also the opposing team, the spectators, and even the referees.

That willpower in action really impressed me, especially since desire and commitment are so important in ultra events. There is a certain amount of technique involved in running, but as the distances get longer, the race depends more on the heart than on the legs. In 15 minutes, I could tell you everything you need to know about the mechanics of running. But I doubt that I could verbalize the X factor that really makes the difference in an ultra event. It's a lot easier to recognize it than it is to define it.

A few facts about ultrarunning need to be understood to be able to appreciate any runner's specific strong points. In the United States, for example, most ultra races are run on trails. In Europe, running on a closed course or a track is much more common. Often the purpose of European track events is not to defeat other runners but rather to set a specific record of time or distance, like running for 48 hours or for 300 miles.

I'm a bit unusual in that I have run both trail races and closed-course events. I'm not the only one who has the ability to do both kinds of events; there simply aren't many others who have chosen to do them. That's unfortunate, because I'm sure many American runners could do really well on the track. I think many U.S. ultrarunners don't even want to try that kind of race because they assume it will be boring to just do endless circuits with no changing scenery. There's also been a tendency in America to look down on track events as mere stunts. Believe me, you can't motivate yourself to run 300 miles just as a stunt.

I hope that track events will become more popular in the United States and that trail running becomes better known in other parts of the world. Until that happens, even some of the best ultrarunners won't develop as much versatility as they might.

Another runner who has done both kinds of racing is Monica Scholz from Ottawa, Ontario. Monica ran 24 100-mile races in a single year. That was an amazing accomplishment, and I was really glad to be able to run with her in the last event of that series. Monica usually starts slowly and then seems to get stronger as the race goes on. In the 2004 Badwater race, her powerful move toward the end of the race allowed her to beat me and emerge as the winning woman. I also really admire Monica as a person. She's always upbeat, and everyone likes to be around her. Somehow, even with all of her running, she has a full-time practice as a divorce lawyer in Canada. She also happens to be legally blind.

For a combination of talent and desire, probably no ultrarunner has matched Ann Trason. She won the Western States 100-miler 14 times—10 times in a row, and 14 out of 15 years. She also holds the women's course record, which she set in 1994.

And consider this: Even for very experienced athletes, running 50 or 60 miles is a challenge, as is running 7-minute miles. In 1995, Ann Trason did a 100-kilometer event (62 miles) at a pace of 6:44 per mile. That means she ran for 7 hours at a speed that many runners couldn't sustain for even a fraction of that time.

Even after she ruptured her hamstring and spent time in a leg cast, Ann came back and won Western States again. In 1998, she and I both completed the grand slam of ultrarunning: four 100-mile runs between June and September.

Ann and I both ran Western States, Leadville, and Wasatch, and Ann was the winning woman each time. Her fourth was a 100-mile race in Vermont, which she also won. I ran the Old Dominion 100 instead. I was exhausted for a year after completing the grand slam, and I hadn't faced the injuries that Ann had dealt with. I don't know if she ever regained top form after the grand slam, but the record she compiled in events all over the world will always place her at the top of ultrarunning. When she was at her peak, Ann was far ahead of all the other women. It's hard to imagine that there will ever be a better runner.

Among the male runners, Scott Jurek really impressed me by making the transition from trail running to the pavement of Badwater in 2005. He had never done a race like Badwater before, and he not only won but also set a new record. When you look at Scott, you can see that he's a natural athlete who could probably be outstanding in lots of different sports. Besides his obvious great strength and speed, he also seems to be able to stay basically relaxed during competition, even when things aren't going especially well. Even though he broke the record at Badwater, I know he endured some hard moments in the heat. Through it all, however, he kept his composure. Scott is just in his early thirties, so he obviously has a great future in ultrarunning.

Without a doubt, the greatest veteran ultrarunner is Marshall Ulrich, who is now in his midfifties. Marshall has run more than 100 races of more than 100 miles in length. He's won Badwater four times, and he once ran across Death Valley four times, for a total of 586 miles. The Leadville Trail 100 in Colorado is one of the most demanding races in the world, and Marshall completed both Leadville and the Pikes Peak Marathon in one weekend. In 1989, he was the first person to complete all six 100-mile trail races in the same year, and he finished in the top 10 in five of them. Marshall is also an accomplished mountain climber who has reached the summit of the tallest peaks on each of the seven continents, including Mount Everest in Asia and Mount Vinson Massif in Antarctica. After all this, Marshall now says he's going to back off from competing in ultra events. We'll see.

Finally, Dean Karnazes has meant a lot to our sport in a number of ways. He's done some great events: winning the 2004 Badwater, for example, and running 350 miles nonstop. He's probably best known for running, by himself, the entirety of The Relay, a 199-mile race from Calistoga to Santa Cruz in California that usually is run by 12-person teams. He's also been a great media spokesperson about ultrarunning.

For a while, because we'd both staked a claim at Badwater, it looked as if there was a rivalry between Dean and me. Even if we were rivals, I never felt that it was in any way a personal conflict. In athletics, sometimes—maybe even most of the time—the greatest accomplishments arise from competition between individuals who seem to be working against each other but who are really collaborating to bring out each person's best. Dean is one of several people who have helped me to go the extra mile, but it's not like we're out to get one another. Athletes are inherently competitive people. Ultimately, though, you compete against yourself. In that sense, any really challenging opponent is also a good friend.

I would be remiss if I didn't mention four great runners who were among my teammates in the 2005 American National 24-Hour Run Championship. Each is a bit unique among American runners for his or her extensive experience in running on tracks. Roy Pirrung has 19 masters ultra championship titles and 28 national ultra championships. He once won a 100-mile race by passing the leader at mile 97, where the lead almost never changes hands. Stephanie Ehret has done many 100-mile events, 24-hour runs, and multiday races. She has been the overall winner in four ultras and the first-place woman in 19, and she's set eight course records. Sandy Powell is the only woman to score for the American team in three World 24-Hour Run events, and she is a two-time silver medalist in the American National 24-Hour Run Championship. John Geesler is a three-time American National 24-Hour Run champion and was the top American in the 2004 World 24-Hour Run, and he has held the American record for the 48-hour run. In 2003 he won the Men's Masters Ultrarunner of the Year Award after running 176.7 miles at the Houston Ultras 48-hour race.

As I said, I'm not a natural spectator. Writing even brief profiles of these great athletes (and they really are great) has been a new experience for me. With a few exceptions—like when I was worried that Monica was going to overtake me in Badwater 2005—I don't think about other runners when I'm in an event. When I first started running, I always assumed someone else would win, and I didn't worry very much about whom that might be. When I became good enough that I might be the winner, I was too focused on the technical side of my own performance to think about the competition. And when I'm not actually in an event, there's too much going on at home and in my work to keep up with other runners' achievements. That's something I might like to change about myself, because it really is important to see what other people have done. My natural inclination is to turn those accomplishments into inspirational fuel for making myself better. I'd also like to learn to just appreciate others' achievements for their own sake.

CHAPTER 19

I DON'T LIKE TO RUN
LONG DISTANCES

People often ask me what I think about when I'm running for so
many hours at a time. The answer isn't very exciting. Usually
I'm concerned about eating and drinking the right amounts so I
don't run out of gas. I never try to keep track of my time during a
race. In fact, I don't even want to know what my pace is or whether
I'm going fast or slow. For some reason, I do wear a watch that I try
not to look at. If I do happen to see it, I feel really frustrated.

An example of this was when I finally did the Hawaiian Ironman
in 1993, 3 years after Jim and I did the Canadian Ironman. In
Canada, I'd done the course in 10:25, which at the time placed me in
the top 10 for one of these competitions—that is, in the money. So
for Hawaii I was registered as a pro. (This basically was a matter of
just applying and paying.) Naturally, I hoped to live up to the
designation.

Unfortunately, my swim was not that fast. I'd hoped to get

around a 1:08. As I got out of the water, there was a *huge* clock that read 1:16. It was only 8 minutes off my goal, but that totally psyched me out. Mentally, I died. Then, as I got on my bike and went on, a woman pedaling near me started going on about how I was "drafting" off her. She said, "You give pros a bad name." I don't even know *how* to draft. It was just so weird, and it brought me even further down.

My bike time was okay, but not great. In the end, I came in 25th among the pros. The irony is that if I'd just done the race without the pro designation, I'd have placed in my age group. It was that stupid big clock that started my downhill mental spiral. So I tend to avoid looking at the time. I don't want to know.

No matter how daunting a race might be, I start out trying to convince myself that it's "obstacle free." There are always lots of problems if you know where to look for them. And if you can't find them, you can always create them. Then it doesn't take long to turn the problem into an excuse. I try hard to resist making obstacles for myself, because I know it can be a powerful and seductive process. I don't want it to get started.

To illustrate this, let me pick on my husband: Jim woke up one morning and said, "It's really hot in here. We need to turn up the air-conditioning."

I looked at the thermostat. The temperature was about 70 degrees. It certainly wasn't hot, but the process was already under way. From Jim's perception that the temperature was too high, it was a short step for him to reach "I can't believe how hot it is in Tucson."

Next came "We've got to move out of Tucson. We've been here way too long. We're leaving. We're leaving now. Let's sell the house!"

It all started with a little thing, an overheated room—which was completely imaginary, by the way. Once you set out on a path like that, you can go as far as you want. You can feel sorry for yourself. You can blame other people. You can whine. You can quit. You can retire to the North Pole if being cool is what makes you happy.

So I try to stay away from negative thoughts. At the same time, I'm not really into "thinking positive" either. Aside from keeping track of food and drink, my ideal mental state in a race is not thinking about anything. If I can get into a zone where it all seems to be happening by itself, I don't have to call on any special thoughts or feelings to get me through. In order to make this happen, I try to run the race in my head beforehand. I visualize the course and imagine myself at different points. Needless to say, this only works when I know what the course will look like.

On a few occasions, I've been able to get into a zone of running that makes it all seem effortless. In 2001, I ran the St. George Marathon in Utah in 2:59, my best time ever. I felt like I was flying. Just a week earlier I had run 3:09 in a marathon in Portland, so cutting 10 minutes off my time was a real surprise. I wish I knew how to make this happen consistently, but I don't.

It's important for me to try to get into a zone because I have never really liked long distances. And in my own mind, I never really run them.

When I was on the track team in high school, sometimes we'd have to run through the streets around the school for fairly long distances. I used to take shortcuts, not so I would be the first one back, but just because I'd get bored with running. It was just practice, so I didn't feel like I was doing anything wrong. Really, I was just trying to make the run more interesting for myself.

I still like to do that, to play little mental tricks on myself during an event. Now those tricks are not just for fun. They're actually a necessity. I don't think anyone, myself included, can just hit the road and run hundreds of miles again and again and not burn out.

Coming from someone who's done so many ultra events, that

may sound surprising. But it's true. In fact, not liking to run long distances is actually why I've been able to run 100-mile races. Along with the necessary physical conditioning, I've had to develop mental tools to overcome my inner resistance to running. I do need to run. That doesn't mean I don't fight it. So I have to psych myself up.

When I compete in a 100-mile race, for instance, I do it 1 mile at a time. In my own mind, I'm not really running 100 miles. I'm running 1 mile 100 times, which to me, as weird as it may sound, is something very different.

I don't think about how many miles I still need to go. Instead, I look at a telephone pole or another landmark up ahead and concentrate on running to that point, and then to another point after that. My mind has to engage in all sorts of negotiations with my body—and both are trying to get the best deal they can!

I think all ultrarunners use some variation of this technique. Without it, I don't think anyone could run extreme distances— certainly not more than once or twice.

Learning how to break down a long distance into a series of much smaller ones is really a key method for getting through any long journey. When a plane flies across the country, for instance, it doesn't just travel in a straight line. It's always being blown off course in one direction or another. So at any given moment, the pilot isn't thinking about how to get from New York to Los Angeles in 6 hours. He's thinking about how to bring the plane back onto the flight path within the next 5 minutes. Of course, the plane will immediately deviate again, maybe in the other direction, and then the correction process has to be repeated. Meanwhile, the overall trip is taking place almost without anyone even thinking about it. The pilot's job is always to look ahead but never to look too far ahead.

This takes mental discipline. It's almost a form of self-hypnosis.

Before a long run, there's a sudden realization of how impossibly far you have to go. So you have to step back from the long-range perspective and just focus on letting the first mile happen, or the first quarter mile, or even the first step.

This is a pretty simple concept that takes real mental toughness to implement. I've noticed that young runners have a hard time with it. Even when some people are in their late twenties and thirties, they can't find the patience and perspective that long-distance running demands. They get intimidated by how far they're trying to go, or they get bored with the time it takes, or they follow some other negative idea to its logical conclusion—that conclusion being that their feet stop moving.

Learning to break things down is one of the most valuable lessons I've learned as an ultrarunner. It's helped me when I feel like I can't sit still, and it's also helped me when I feel like I can't get going. When I'm really wired, I convince myself that everything needs to happen at once. The worst part of it is that I actually believe that that's possible. I want everything to happen now, and I can't understand why everybody else doesn't feel the same way. This somewhat irrational impatience is also why I used to get angry with the girls on my tennis team back in college. It seemed so obvious that we should be practicing and that anything else was a waste of time.

The opposite of this comes when I think I can't do anything—not just running, but anything. I'll walk into a room of our house and it will be really messy. Probably, there are just a few things lying around, but to me it looks completely trashed. And it seems like there's nothing I can do about it. I can't even begin to start cleaning it up. I want to, but I can't. It's all too overwhelming and it'll just get messed up again, so what would be the point?

In both cases, the trick is to do less than I think I have to do. I don't have to get to the finish line this instant; I just have to get to that next bend in the road. I don't have to clean up the whole house; I just have to put one object back where it belongs.

Once again, training yourself to think in bite-size bits takes practice and willpower. But it's something you've really got to learn if you want to be a long-distance runner, or the mom of a house full of kids.

I've also developed a way to use this tool in reverse. Instead of tricking myself by making something seem smaller or shorter than it is, I trick myself with the idea of something larger or longer. I'll tell myself, "Well, Pam, you're going to run 15 miles this morning, so you'd better get started."

Then the same old thoughts appear: "Fifteen miles! I must be crazy! I don't even want to *drive* 15 miles!" So I negotiate with myself: "Pam, you don't have to run all 15 miles at one time. That's just too far. So I'll tell you what. You can run half in the morning and half in the afternoon. What a great deal! Go for it!"

Tricks like these can help with the most difficult part of running—the most difficult part of anything, really—conquering it in your mind's eye. If you can mentally convince yourself that you can tackle a task, whether it's running a marathon or cleaning up a room, you can always accomplish it physically.

Well, maybe not always. Almost always. Often. More often than you think. Sometimes, at least. Definitely sometimes!

CHAPTER 20

MY BRAIN, PART THREE:
I'M IN CONTROL

Here are some final thoughts on anorexia. I'm not an expert, and I don't have much faith in the experts on this problem. When I was in the hospital, the basic approach was to cast patients as victims. The only real question was, Who should take the blame? Usually it seemed to be the parents. Sometimes, it was suggested, it might be a sexual abuser whom the patient couldn't necessarily identify or even consciously remember. I think the intention of this "blame game" may have been positive. It was supposed to relieve us of whatever guilt we may have felt by locating the cause of anorexia somewhere outside ourselves.

I really didn't find this method acceptable. I believe that I am responsible for whatever I do. If I feel guilt for my actions, I just have to live with it instead of trying to make my actions the fault of someone else. Freedom from guilt isn't worth the price of portraying myself as a basically passive human being.

Talking with other patients in the hospital was really a contradictory experience. No one wanted to talk about anorexia because that topic was always being worked by the staff. Patients had conventional conversations on conventional subjects. Everyone seemed quite normal. At the same time, I felt that everyone else was in worse shape than I was. The other patients seemed normal, except for one area of their lives. Maybe they were even "excessively normal," as a way of compensating for whatever was wrong. And their problems seemed deeper than mine.

I've given talks on anorexia at schools and colleges, but I don't have answers to the problem. What I do have is experience and some suggestions. One difficulty with anorexia is the fact that it's fundamentally a mental problem. The physical symptoms come from a reality that exists in somebody's head, and getting into somebody's head isn't easy. Even people with anorexia don't like to face this fact. To put it bluntly, it's easier to think of yourself as physically sick than to think of yourself as crazy.

Yet anorexia expresses itself as crazy behavior. There were times when I was suicidal, and it wasn't because I was depressed. My body chemistry had become so unstable that my mind ran away from me. All kinds of weird things were going on. I was getting lots of speeding tickets and parking tickets. Someone could have punched me really hard and I'm sure I wouldn't have felt it. I was out of touch with myself and with the world, both literally and figuratively.

When anorexia can make people feel that way—as it has hundreds of thousands of individuals—there's no doubt that it's a major problem for society. Any advice or insight I can offer, however, has to be from a very personal viewpoint. If a parent were to ask me how to deal with an eating disorder in a child, I would have to look back at my own childhood and adolescence. I'm certain that my father and mother wanted what was best for me. Now that I'm a parent, I know how easy it is to make mistakes almost *because* you're trying so hard to do the right thing. It must be a terrible feeling to have a child come back 30 years later and tell you about everything you did wrong. I'll never do that.

At the same time, I don't want to take the safe way out by not saying anything at all about my personal history. As I've said, it took a while for anyone in my family to realize that I had a problem. Once they did realize it, the subjects of food and eating quickly became a big deal. Eating stopped being a matter of nutrition, much less pleasure, and turned into a power struggle. The dinner table became a kind of theater where a battle of wills was acted out. Once that got started, things were really on a downward course. I was a relatively small child, and the truth is that I really didn't need all that much food for a healthy diet. My parents' harping on food was supposed to be about my nutritional needs. In reality, those needs quickly got lost in the ego battles.

So if a parent were to ask me for help in dealing with an anorexic child, my first suggestion would be to downgrade the importance given to the child's eating behavior. Or, more accurately, to downgrade the importance that's *outwardly shown* to that behavior. Of course you don't ignore an obvious eating problem in a child, but it's a mistake to push the panic button about it at every possible occasion.

Frustration can really build up. There's nothing more exasperating than knowing you're right and still having someone resist—especially if that someone is your child. I know there are times when parents want to literally shove food down their child's throat. Obviously, that's not going to work. It's taking away control in one of the few areas that kids really feel they have it.

In my opinion, anorexia is about having personal control. It is about eating and food, but foremost it's about personal autonomy.

Especially for a younger person, who may not yet have control over other aspects of her life, this is one area where she can have personal volition. An adolescent may not always make the wisest choices when she is "in control." At first, it has the appeal of a game, with well-defined rules and boundaries. At the start, you can still eat. As the game gets more complicated, you can change the rules and introduce new tactics. It's like Monopoly. You're just moving around the board at the start, and then you begin to build houses and hotels, you cut all sorts of deals, you play more aggressively. The same sequence can be followed in anorexia. You can cut back on your food intake, or even cut it out altogether. At first you may want to do this only during certain periods of the day or on certain days of the week. There are all sorts of variations. The real problem comes, however, when the control issue turns upside down. The sense of power that came from telling yourself "I can eat whenever I want to" is gone. You literally *can't* eat, due to an extreme and uncontrollable revulsion toward food.

Once you understand the extent to which anorexia is about control, you can see what a mistake it is to take control away from an anorexic. It sounds simplistic, but people with this problem will feel very uncomfortable when other people tell them what to put in their mouths. It doesn't matter whether it's hamburgers and mashed potatoes at the dinner table or antidepressant drugs in a psychiatric ward. There's going to be resistance because for an anorexic person, the issue is really integrity, not in the sense of right and wrong but in the sense of a ship's integrity being breached when a leak develops in the hull. It's not an easy thing to explain. It's not easy to understand unless you've actually experienced it. If you have experienced it, it's *still* not easy.

With all this in mind, one thing remains very clear to me. Even if my parents had said and done everything perfectly, I still would have had a serious problem. A 16-year-old girl simply is not going to listen to her mother and father. It doesn't matter if they are the wisest human beings on the face of the earth. People with anorexia need help, but they also need to be ready for it. Most adolescents simply haven't reached that point.

A significant amount of time had to pass before I was going to change. Some very important experiences had to happen. And when change did occur for me, it wasn't in the context of treatment for anorexia. It was in the context of running. When running (which I very much wanted to do) came into conflict with eating (which still made me uncomfortable), something had to give.

I've already described how this came about, when Chuck Giles told me about the Badwater race and explained how important it was to have a sound nutritional plan. Getting enough fuel into the body was simply a prerequisite for competing. When I think about that conversation and the effect it had on me, I'm struck by the fact that I don't think Chuck was even aware of my anorexia at the time. So he wasn't giving a prescription to a sick person; he was giving advice to an athlete. Because of this, my defenses weren't up. Chuck was just giving me the facts, and I made the choice to act accordingly. I was still in control. I was ready, and I was able to put anorexia behind me.

How great that was, but also how sad. Great that Chuck managed to get through to me, even if he had no idea of the larger importance of his message. But sad that it had not happened sooner, not with my parents, not with my doctors, not with people who really loved and cared about me. And there was also an ironic twist to all of this. Anorexia had ruled my life for 15 years and had done a lot of damage in the process. One of its effects had been to condition my body to an amazing degree for ultrarunning. Something that had hurt me at one time in my life would now help me in another.

Does that mean my anorexia was ultimately a good thing? Absolutely not. It was a very bad thing. But it could have been worse.

It's not out of my life completely, and I'm sure it never will be. But at least it's in the background, once and for all.

Game over.

CHAPTER 21

YOU AREN'T
WHAT YOU EAT

After any significant athletic event, the winner is usually interviewed. People immediately want to know the secret of your success—your winning strategy. This is where there is at least one important difference between the questions asked of ultra athletes and those asked of athletes in any other sport.

A key side effect of our sport is a steady burn of calories, so ultra athletes are asked about what they eat: "What did you eat before the race? How about during the race? Will you have a big meal after the race?" And the more detailed the answer, the better. It's as if people think that eventually there will emerge a formula for what makes an endurance athlete competitive—and it'll be put into a bottle or gel pack. Is there some supersubstance that will ensure peak performance, and if so, precisely how many grams of it should an aspiring athlete consume? Or is there a particular regimen that one should follow—a magic combination of slow-burning carbs, protein, and supplements? They all want to know what they should eat so they can run like a miracle—and like a machine.

In ultrarunning, nutrition is taken very, very seriously, much more so than in other sports. After the Super Bowl, no one asks the quarterback how much wheat germ he ate for breakfast. In contrast, after he broke the record at Badwater, Scott Jurek was immediately answering questions about his food intake. From what I read, it seemed that there was a lot of fascination with the fact that Scott doesn't eat any meat.

I suppose this level of interest makes sense. After all, ultra events require a lot of energy, and energy comes from what we eat and drink. That seems reasonable.

That said, even though I've been successful at numerous ultra events, I'm still probably the worst person to answer questions about what to consume for peak results. Except for when I'm actually racing—and to a large degree, even then—I am not very careful about what I eat. I am sure that my history of anorexia is a huge factor in this. I don't really eat much at all, relative to the exertion I'm experiencing. My body seems able and even content to perform with very limited fuel, a fact that once caused my husband to refer to me as a "freak of nature." One of my crew, when asked what I eat, responded simply, "She eats crap."

I actually like an empty feeling. I feel intense hunger for a while, then it goes away and I really don't feel any desire to eat. Of course, that doesn't mean that I don't *need* to eat.

Although it's never been tested, I seem to have a somewhat unusual metabolism that shouldn't be used as a model for other people. It's a mystery even to me.

I can say this: My approach to nutrition and running is probably about as unscientific as you can get. I don't believe in the magical powers of a vegan diet, a high-carb diet, an all-fish diet, or eating an energy bar every 3.5 miles. Running magazines publish a lot of articles about what foods will give the average person a fast burst of energy and which will give a slow release. They'll tell you what is good for your heart, your muscles, and your joints. All of this stuff is good to know simply because it can point you in the right direction to be generally healthy. But it's not the holy grail of performance, because you also read about an ultrarunner who scarfed down a large pizza, a whole cheesecake, tortilla chips, burritos, doughnuts, and a lot of other stuff on a long run. I don't recall seeing any of that chow covered in the "power food" or "healthy supplements" columns in any of my running magazines.

The only generalizing I think it's possible to do is pretty obvious: If you're a smaller person, you don't need to eat as much to keep your system working. If you carry a lot of bulk, it's going to want to be fed. If you make your body work hard, you have to keep it fueled, and a bigger person requires more fuel. Even a smaller person, I've discovered, can't work the body hard on nothing but air.

When I'm not competing, I eat whatever I want. It's nothing exotic. For breakfast I almost always have coffee and a muffin before going for my first run of the day. For dinner I usually have a salad, maybe potatoes of some kind, bread, and perhaps steak or salmon. Typically, I don't eat lunch. I eat candy. I know I won't get a thank-you from the American Dental Association for saying this, but I honestly don't think candy is that bad for you. Not hard candy, anyway, and that's what I like. It's just sugar, and not even that many calories. My favorite is a particular kind of lemon drop that is very sour. The weird thing is that it's the same candy that was loved by my grandfather—the one who walked 300 miles from Wisconsin to Chicago. Maybe there's something in that.

If I'm racing, what I eat really depends on how long the race is. Rather than focusing on what I'll eat during a race, most of the time I start out healthy and strong. If it's a really long race, I might try to put on a few pounds in the weeks leading up to the race. I don't really have any systematic way of doing this. I just start eating a lot more protein, carbs, and fat—everything. It's uncomfortable, but I have to do it because I know I'm going to need that weight. If I'm too light going into a more strenuous race, I dig into my fat stores too early.

Just in the past year or so I've noticed that when my body weight is up 2 or 3 pounds, I can go for a run and lose all of it in one day. I don't think it's a matter of hydration. I think that all my slow running and training has gotten my body used to going immediately to my fat stores.

During the race itself, if it's only a 50-miler, I might not eat at all—just stay hydrated and take on some calories by drinking. Depending on when the race gets going, I might have a can of Ensure just before the start. Once I've had my coffee and muffin, I really don't want any other actual food. I might have a bite of an orange or something like that, if it happens to be handy. Otherwise, for a race of that length I don't think much about food.

For a longer race—one of at least 100 miles—again, my focus is on drinking rather than eating. At some point I'll probably have some oatmeal or mashed potatoes. They fill you up quickly and the energy kicks in fast. I don't feel like messing with a lot of chewing. I could also eat rice or pasta, which would be pretty much the same thing. Potatoes and oatmeal are my preference.

It's a little different for a race on a track, like a 24- or 48-hour race. Then I really do need to have a controlled flow of adequate energy. There just aren't that many other variables that I can use for an edge. I'm not going to knock anyone out because he or she can't take the heat and I can. Being tough on hills is moot when it's a flat track. So the edge pretty much comes down to who can keep herself or himself consistently strong over the duration of the race. I'm totally convinced of that.

You can get really paranoid about food when you do a closed-course race like the 24- or 48-hour events. Everyone can see everyone else. You're all just going around in circles together. You start out with a plan for how you are going to keep yourself fed, then you see someone eating something, something that you don't usually eat or would never even think of eating. You question yourself—oh, should I do that? It's easy to start second-guessing yourself.

As unscientific and casual-to-a-fault as I am about food, I used to be a lot worse. It was only after I met Chuck that I started to be a little more reasonable about my nutrition during events. Chuck was very clear that if I expected to do well I was going to have to change my approach to fueling for a race. He had done research on a lot of different products and he felt that Ensure gave the best bang for the buck. Or rather, it was the most calorie-dense, digestible product, so given that I needed to eat but didn't feel like eating, it seemed to be the ticket.

I was resistant at first, for two reasons.

First of all, in 1991, during my second hospitalization for anorexia, some of the women, those whose weight had fallen to around 75 pounds, were told to drink Ensure. At 330 calories per 8-ounce bottle, it appeared to be the preferred product for desperate cases. I was advised to drink it, too. I couldn't mentally put myself in the same category as those very ill patients. So if it was prescribed for them, I was determined to avoid it.

Then, just before doing my first Badwater, Jim and I were at the Elkhorn 100-K. Because Chuck had been singing the praises of Ensure, Jim had brought some along. He gave me a bottle to try. I immediately vomited. This reaction to nourishment is not at all uncommon during an ultra event, regardless of what you put in your stomach, and it's another reason that I try to eat very little during a race. When you are running, your energy goes mainly into your extremities—the legs and, to some extent, the arms. Not a lot is available for digestion. Even though I knew this was probably why I had gotten sick, vomiting still put me off the Ensure.

Chuck prevailed upon me to give it another try. Since then it's become a mainstay. During my fourth Badwater, I drank 40 cans. Forty cans at 330 calories each—I don't even want to do the math. It's still hard for me to think about consuming such large numbers of calories. But during that race, I didn't lose any weight.

For staying awake, alert, and moderately coherent during longer races, Red Bull energy drink has also been really good for me. It gives a powerful boost without the subsequent crash and burn and dehydration that come with coffee. Also, I really prefer something carbonated like Red Bull. Water feels unbelievably heavy when I'm running. It just lies there in my stomach, sloshing around. If I want just to keep my mouth wet or to replace what I have sweated away, I drink soda water. So Ensure, Red Bull, and soda water are my three nutritional pillars. As I've said, it's not very scientific.

One of the biggest potential problems for ultrarunners is dehydration. When you perspire heavily, your body loses salt, potassium, magnesium, and other minerals called electrolytes. These carry a minute electric charge that helps regulate blood chemistry and muscle action. Electrolyte depletion can cause the shutdown of basic physiological systems. In really long races, electrolyte replacement can be a critical factor. Drinking plain water does not replenish electrolytes, so most people need a sports drink like Gatorade, Amino Vital, or another electrolyte drink to replenish the lost salts and minerals. There are also capsules that can be taken with water.

The conventional wisdom on how much to drink during a race has changed in recent years. Dehydration used to be the big worry. Lately there have been some studies and a lot of articles about the opposite phenomenon—too much liquid, specifically water, not containing any replacement salts or electrolytes. When you drink too much water and sweat out all your body salts, your blood can become diluted. This is called hyponatremia. Then your body tries to equalize the sodium concentrations in your blood and tissue cells. This can cause swelling in the brain, and there have even been reports of coma and death—not good.

In my opinion, a main reason that this problem has gotten bad enough to attract this much attention is that marathons are quickly gaining in popularity. Many people who run marathons these days are not seasoned runners. They don't understand that the reason there tend to be lots of aid stations handing out water is so that runners can pace their intake individually. The presence of a station every mile or two is not a recommendation that you drink that frequently, every time you see a table full of cups. You probably need less fluid than that unless weather conditions are extreme. Runners need to learn to listen to their bodies. (Because of this issue, there is now a trend among race directors to have fewer aid stations at races.)

I don't think I'm at much risk of developing hyponatremia because I don't drink that much straight water when I'm racing. At Badwater, I take in some kind of fluid every 2 minutes because it's *so* dry. When I'm not in a race across Death Valley, I might drink 16 ounces over the course of 30 miles.

The crew is really important during a long race. They are the ones who keep tabs on how much I'm eating. They make me eat or drink even when I don't feel like it. Sometimes it feels like they're bashing me. I feel like a kid who doesn't want to be told what to do, especially when it's been hours and hours and they're giving me my 30th can of Ensure or Red Bull or whatever. I *really* don't want it. And even though I know it's for my own good, I get mad. Susy always tries to be sweet and reasonable with me. She'll say, "If you don't want it, Pam, you don't have to drink it." All the while, though, she's figuring out how to make me drink it.

Without the crew, I would totally misgauge my intake. During my first Badwater, I think all I ate was a few bites of a peanut butter sandwich and some Ultra Fuel slushies, if the latter can be counted as semisolid food. In other races I've either forgotten to eat or resisted having food pushed on me. The fourth time I ran Badwater, I felt like I couldn't drink any more—imagine drinking every 2 minutes for more than 24 hours—or eat anything. Susy and Chuck kept nagging me, and I was really irritable. We were at the bottom of the pass and they kept pressing me to drink. I was like, "I can't." Finally there was barely more than a mile to go. The crew went to park the van and wait for me, and suddenly I was *starving.* I had this emptiness in my gut; I was light-headed. I had the feeling I couldn't take another step. So I wanted to be fed. Chuck went to the van and found me a cookie. I ate a few bites—about half the cookie. It kicked in almost immediately and I was able to finish the race.

After a race, it's supposed to be very important to get food back into your system. Sometimes I'm really dying to have a meal after I finish. Other times the prolonged exertion seems to blunt my sense of taste. Everything I eat seems totally bland, like sawdust. Want a sawdust sandwich, Pam? No, thank you.

I honestly believe—in spite of my issues with food—that nutrition is the single biggest factor in a race. And yet, in the 14 or 15 years I've been racing, I've learned that people are not like cars, performing pretty predictably based upon what we put in them. Yes, we are like cars in that we need fuel, and better "fuel" should better our performance. However, it's also true that you could always eat the same thing and, on any given day, it'll work differently. There's just no way to predict, for sure, the reaction and result you'll get. This, to me, is the most frustrating part. Even though I've made some comments here about what has worked for me in the past, on any given day that very thing might *not* work for me. Every person has to experiment to find out what *usually* works, and then understand that a day will likely come when it won't.

CHAPTER 22

BADWATER 3: REALLY BAD

After my second consecutive Badwater victory, it was not just other ultrarunners who had me in their radar, so to speak. A number of articles were written about my win, and I was even invited to be a guest on the *Late Show with David Letterman*. David made some pretty good jokes at my expense. The best was his expression of disbelief that anyone would be crazy enough to run 135 miles through the scorching desert for a belt buckle! It was a lot of fun for my family to go to New York; Jim and I took four of the boys, and I got to run in Central Park for the first time.

Late in the winter of 2003, Jim and I went skiing in Utah. While we were there, I got a call from a producer for the Discovery Channel. They wanted to do a piece on my next Badwater race. At that point, I wasn't even signed up for Badwater. Being on the Discovery Channel sounded exciting, though.

The producer had a particular concept in mind: He wanted Jim to do the race, too, with each of us wearing a device to measure our vital functions. The idea was to compare the physiological reactions of a man and a woman.

I didn't think Jim would be in shape to do Badwater. He did toy with the idea for about 10 minutes. As for me, although I hadn't exactly been planning to do the race a third time, now I wanted to.

From its inception, Badwater 2004 was a media event, and it just kept getting bigger. In May I got an e-mail from a producer at *60 Minutes*. The venerable TV newsmagazine also wanted to film me at Badwater. Wow, this was amazing. Then I heard from the Nature Channel. And *The New York Times* was also going to be there. Needless to say, I had never before been the focus of this much attention. I'm not sure that *any* ultrarunner had been.

Chuck had been enthusiastic about the Discovery Channel's interest, but as other media outlets began to get involved, his reaction became more tempered. He cautioned me that all this attention might not be the best idea considering that I was trying to accomplish something serious. But it wasn't like I could keep the media away, even if I had wanted to. It was really beyond my control.

Once I had committed to it, I trained very hard for the race. There were some (notably Chuck and Jim) who felt I was training too hard, and especially that I was doing too many long runs before Badwater. Just 6 weeks before, I ran 212 miles in the 48-hour run in France, taking the record for American women in my age group. Then I did Western States, another 100-mile race, just a couple of weeks before Badwater. I was also doing 22-mile training runs up and down the Santa Catalina Mountains in Tucson. I really wanted to be ready for whatever Badwater would hold. My third effort was beginning to seem like a very big deal.

The day before the race, there was a bit of Hollywood melodrama as Dean Karnazes went limping around in an ankle brace, as if he wasn't sure he would be able to start. I guess that was intended to psych out his competition. He and I were again in the last flight of starters. Sure enough, when it was time to go, Dean took off like a rabbit.

In past years we'd had to provide our own transportation. This year my local Ford dealers, Dan Newton and Jim Click, provided us with two vans decorated with colorful Ford decals as well as my name and bib number: number 1. Dean Karnazes, Monica Scholz, and Chris Bergland also had colorful decals on their vehicles. Elite runners from Russia, Germany, and Brazil were there. And of course there was way more of a press presence than in the past, giving the whole thing a circuslike atmosphere.

Although I'd thought I was ready, I couldn't get my head into the race at all. The race date had been moved up to the first week in July, which made a noticeable difference in the temperature. A lot of the other runners were commenting on how cool it was, relatively speaking. Meanwhile I, who usually see higher heat as an advantage, was boiling hot right from the start. I really didn't feel well. After 40 miles I still had no rhythm. I told the people from *60 Minutes* that they probably wouldn't even want to use the film they were shooting, since I was tanking the race so badly. They said, "Oh, no. This is fine!" I knew they couldn't believe how hot it was. They should have filmed themselves.

I have to say, my crew was as great as ever. Craig was back. He'd recently gotten married and his wife, Stephanie, was also crewing. Susy was back for her third time, and Chuck was there, of course. Everybody wanted to be there, and everybody gave 100 percent.

Even though I didn't feel right, I wasn't doing that badly. Ferg Hawke, a veteran ultrarunner from Canada, had the lead at the halfway mark. I wasn't that concerned about him. I knew that this was the first time he'd done the race, so there was a good chance that he had underestimated what it would take to keep going. I figured I would catch him.

I was more worried about Dean, who was also ahead of me and was considered the underdog—if you could call someone who'd competed so strongly the year before an underdog. All I could do was run my own race and hope he fell apart.

Suddenly, at around mile 90, I got my period. Now there's something for the Nature Channel! This I had not planned for. I felt like I was going to vomit. Luckily, *60 Minutes* was nice enough not to film that bit.

For this race, there was lots of media attention— Discovery, *60 Minutes*—a circus. The first race there was only NPR. All the interaction with the runners—it was a little out of line, though I don't think out of character, in some respects. Like, it's 2:00 a.m. in the Mojave Desert, not a soul for miles. Peace is all-consuming. Then a van speeds up beside you and puts a big spotlight on you, and someone starts barking questions. What? Did an alien craft just land? They weren't badgering, but it's still somewhat disconcerting. It takes so much just to focus to do the race; to do one more thing is just impossible. Pam, though, was very cordial, even though I don't think she was thrilled.

—*Craig Bellmann*

The most deflating moment was when Monica passed me. We had seen her coming—my crew had watched her vans approaching. She was in such good condition, so solid. It was clear she could keep going like that all the way to the finish. She got a 50-minute lead. By the time I got to Mount Whitney, I knew I was going to finish fourth, behind Dean, Ferg, and Monica.

Not being the winning woman was kind of a disappointment. Monica had a really great race and deserved the win. Dean also ran a great race. I totally have to hand it to him. When he needed to be good, he performed.

There was a bit of irony in the circumstances of Dean's win. I read in Dean's book, *Ultramarathon Man*, that after a friend of his had gotten pretty beat up doing a 50-miler, Dean had jokingly sent him a tampon, implying, I guess, that the friend "ran like a girl." Well, I guess Dean did prove that when a girl has her period, he can beat her!

I'd like to think that part of the story at Badwater 2004 was that in a field that was 90 percent men, two women were in the top four. In the weeks leading up to the race I had received a lot of encouraging calls and e-mails from many of my running friends and from women and teenagers I didn't even know. I hope none of them was disappointed with my effort, even if the result was not what we'd hoped it would be.

CHAPTER 23

YOU'RE ONLY A
VIRGIN ONCE

O ver the past several years, since I've made something of a mark in my sport, I've had runners take the time to tell me that I have inspired them in some way. It feels great to be appreciated. Often, these people ask me for tips. I don't feel completely comfortable giving advice about a sport in which the exception always seems to be the rule. Yet although my story here is not exactly a "how-to," the odd suggestion may be gleaned from these pages ("odd" being the operative word).

So here is tip number one for any new distance runner: Savor the milestones.

In your running career, whether you compete at the top level or just make running an enjoyable part of a long, healthy life, you are only a virgin once. Only once will you run your first 10-K, your first half-marathon, your first full marathon, your first ultra. So when you do experience a first, I think that it's really important to stop for a moment to recognize how great it feels—whether you just give yourself a pat on the back or throw yourself a party.

I say this in hindsight since I didn't really do it enough myself. Everything was so exciting when I first started. All I cared about was running as much as I possibly could. I would finish one event and think, "Well, when's the next one?" Whenever it was, wherever it was, I would try to get there just to be on a course again.

Now I've run more than 100 marathons. I've run some of them 10 times. I've also done well over 100 ultra events of distances ranging from 50 to 300 miles. I still don't like to miss a major event, even if it's not one of my favorites. In fact, some of the ones I most enjoy aren't at all widely known. Anyone who continues participating in this sport will develop personal preferences. The events I mention in this chapter are my own choices, but I do strongly recommend them. They offer the challenges I'm looking for and also another element that I'm coming to value more: I want an event that's physically and mentally demanding without being stressful in the way that everyday life is. I can get enough of that elsewhere. When I'm running, I want to get where I want to go—which is not to the supermarket, the car wash, or the veterinarian.

I've already mentioned the **Holualoa Tucson Marathon** in the beautiful Santa Catalina Mountains. Because it's my baby, I'm partial to this one even though, as director of the full marathon, it's hard work for me and I don't get to run the race. I recommend it for beginners and anyone who does not like to climb, because it's all downhill. Some runners have posted their fastest personal times on this course, and a lot of people qualify for the Boston Marathon.

The **St. George Marathon** in Utah will always be very important to me because I have recorded some of my best times there. And at least the first time I ran it, my result seemed serendipitous—completely unexpected. In 2000, I had had some pretty significant oral surgery but wanted to attend this event anyway, partially to promote the Tucson Marathon. I'd decided that I would take it easy on the run so my mouth wouldn't start bleeding. Instead, I'd devote most of my energy to distributing the flyers that I'd brought along. The night before, I spent about 3 hours in the whirlpool at my hotel; I didn't sleep especially well. The next day, as planned, I was taking it easy, occasionally chatting with someone running near me. About halfway through the race, someone happened to mention that we were running at a sub-3-hour pace. I didn't have the sense that we were going that fast, so I didn't take it seriously at first. A short while later, I was running near a woman whom I guessed to be in her fifties. I commented that she seemed to be pretty good, and a man nearby said that she was attempting to break the world record for her age group. When yet another runner commented that we could break 3 hours, it finally sank in. At that point I started running as hard as I could. I crossed the finish at 3:00:11.

The following year I had just done the Portland Marathon in a time of 3:09 a week before when I found myself at St. George again. Jim and I were talking about the close-but-no-cigar finish the previous year, and he said that it was too bad that I'd just done Portland because if I hadn't had that exertion I might be able to break 3 hours at St. George. Well, even with Portland at my back, in 2001 I got in just under the wire, crossing the finish line in 2:59.

The St. George course is mostly downhill and steep. The race takes place in the fall, so temperature is not a problem. This is a really beautiful course, though somewhat out of the way—about 2 hours north of Las Vegas and 4 hours south of Salt Lake City. It's a really good marathon for a first-timer.

Two other rural marathons I like are the **Big Sur Marathon** in California and the **Lost Dutchman Marathon** just outside Phoenix, where I was the winning woman in 2002. Most people find these courses more difficult than St. George. Although they're not killers, they're moderately hard. I like the fact that they're a little out of the way. For the same reason, I used to like the **Mule Mountain Marathon** near Tucson. Unfortunately, it's no longer being run. One thing that must be said of Big Sur: It's the most beautiful marathon I've ever done. You run north on Highway 1, with the ocean to your left and the mountains to your right. As you run, you can hear seals calling to one another on the rocks below. I was literally running with tears in my eyes. It's just gorgeous. That, right there, is reason enough to live in California.

Among better-known events, the **Chicago Marathon** has always been a good experience for me. Chicago is also an excellent first marathon because the course is so flat. Except for a couple of slightly sloping bridges over the Chicago River, there's not a hill in the whole 26 miles. The marathon takes place in October. Considering Chicago's climate, it's almost eerie how mild the weather has been year after year. I've always loved Chicago.

The **Boston Marathon** is the gold-standard event of American running, and it deserves to be. As a race director, I appreciate the work that the whole city puts into this race. There was a huge marathon craze in the United States in the 1970s, and then it more or less died out until the early 1990s—except in Boston, where it never died down. When you run this event, you're continuing a tradition, because it's much older than any other American marathon. It has some tough hills near the end of the course, but the first obstacle you have to overcome is getting a qualifying time to be eligible to run the race. You have to run other marathons before running Boston, which I think is a good thing. It forces you to develop yourself as a runner. So, there is a high level of seriousness in the athletes who compete. Another neat thing about Boston is that the fans watching the race feed you. As you're running along, people hand you drinks and energy bars and popsicles. It's great.

I also really like the **Flora London Marathon**. No big-city marathon is more impressive. It's huge—40,000 people do the race, with three different starting locations that all come together at mile 8. And it's a very fast course, very smooth. I have to give a big hand to the race organizers—it's just terrifically well done.

Aside from the physical settings, there are some big psychological differences between events like Boston and Chicago and the rural marathons. Most people are used to running by themselves or with one or two other people. You can trot along, get lost in your thoughts, or have a pleasant conversation. In an event like Chicago, you suddenly find yourself being stared at and yelled at by thousands of people. The cheering crowds are definitely encouraging, but it's a hugely different experience from the kind of running I usually do. This is where the concept of "running within yourself" becomes important. I need to filter out distractions and keep focused on my goals. You'd be surprised how difficult this can be when you're part of a crowd of runners on a narrow street, with a tremendous racket echoing off the buildings on either side. It can be exhilarating, but some runners—myself included—also find it disturbing. Be prepared for that if you choose to do an event in a major city.

I'm not a purist when it comes to marathons. Things change. When I first started running, there was an intensity about marathons that has really been diluted. It used to be that pretty much everyone in the race was really ready to bust a gut. They saw themselves as elite—average Joes and Janes did not feel capable of getting up in the morning and running 26 miles. The atmosphere is a lot more casual now. In 2004, 36,000 people completed the ING New York City Marathon. How elite can it be? I've run the Los Angeles Marathon three times and seen runners carrying pizzas, runners dressed as Ronald McDonald, and runners running backward. You have to be in the right mood for that kind of thing. I wasn't offended.

Some runners really enjoy a party atmosphere with their race. For them, the **Rock 'n' Roll Marathon** in San Diego, which takes place in June, is hard to beat. There's a different rock band every mile, plus 40 squads of cheerleaders. This actually might be closer to what the first marathons were like in ancient Greece, when athletics were both competition and celebration. In any case, marathon organizers today frequently look for ways to be uniquely appealing. They want to have big turnouts, and they want the runners to do well. In my opinion, having a band every mile is pretty much moot. If you are actually running the race, you hear a couple of chords and you're already past the band. It's great for the spectators, though.

I really have to give credit to the organizers. After the success of the San Diego event, they started up a sister marathon in the Phoenix area that I think was the biggest first-time event ever. People attending these events are really going to have a good time. They know they don't have to get a 3:15 time; 4:15 or a bit slower is closer to the average. I know a lot of women like to do this kind of event together. They have dinner, maybe see a show, have some getaway time, all planned around a nice run.

The biggest change in marathons, especially in New York, Chicago, and Los Angeles, has been the thousands of people who are now *walking*. This would have been unthinkable a few years ago. Walking was a sign of defeat. It was embarrassing. But that view only takes the elite athlete into account. Over the past several years the idea of what a marathon is has evolved, or maybe its appeal has simply broadened. It was always a symbol of accomplishment. Now that symbol is being sought by so many others—older people who want to prove that they still have a lot of life left in them; disabled people or veterans with permanent injuries who say, "I still can do it"; or even just people making a commitment to take better care of themselves. For me, it would be more difficult to walk the course than to run it. However, I can only applaud those who want to get out there and do their 26 miles in any way they are able. I know that in the same way that Badwater was a life-altering experience for me, walking a marathon is a life-altering experience for others. I'm not going to get any more out of it than they are just because I run and they walk.

You may not believe this, but I've never run the ING New York City Marathon. This is not from lack of desire. It's run only a few weeks before the Tucson Marathon, and at that time of year I'm usually up to my eyeballs in stuff that needs to be taken care of. However, I've finally decided to bite the bullet and hire some help for Elisa and myself to organize the marathon. That will make it possible for me to run in New York. I'm looking forward to it. I mean, how cool is that, to have been doing marathons for so long and still to have such a big cherry left?

Oh, did I say that you're only a virgin once? What I meant was *each time.* That's because the milestones you can set for yourself are really limitless. There's not only your first marathon but also your first *Boston* or your first *international* marathon. And then, if you choose to do something crazy, your first ultra. My 300-miles-without-sleeping run, though certainly grueling, was wonderful because I'd never done it before. (So we don't get too far off the subject, I'll tell you more about that one in the next chapter.)

Not for the faint of heart, all ultras feature challenge, struggle, and pain, but some more so than others. Probably the most extreme is the **Hardrock Hundred Mile Endurance Run** in Silverton, Colorado. Obviously, this is a long race, but the length is only part of its difficulty. It's not called the Hardrock for nothing. Generally, I do well on difficult courses, but in this one the altitude is just too high for me. My husband loves this event, even though he hasn't yet been able to complete it.

Two ultras in the same category as Hardrock are the **Western States 100**, in Northern California, and the **Leadville Trail 100**, in Colorado. I've done Western States many times. Even though the course isn't really suited to me, I keep going back because it's a great event. It's like the Boston and the Ironman of ultras. Because I'm not as strong in this race, and because Western States happens just 2 weeks before Badwater, which is practically my signature race, in the past few years I've tended to think of the former as a warmup. No doubt that has affected my performance. Sometimes having Badwater on the horizon helped me do well at Western States because I was really relaxed. Other times it hurt me because I wasn't as focused as I like to be. This race has a ton of downhill mileage, so if you're a good downhill trail runner, you can do well here.

Leadville is the other slice of bread in the Badwater sandwich. Needless to say, after doing two major races just before I get to Leadville, I'm in a very different state of mind and body than normally. I've done the race seven times, finishing five times and dropping out twice. I really like the town of Leadville and the event's atmosphere. I'm sure I'll be going back. It may not be quite as difficult as Hardrock, but parts of Leadville are very hard mentally. Toward the end there's a steep climb up Sugarloaf Mountain and then a descent. It takes focus and commitment. I dropped out in 2005 because I just wasn't sufficiently into it to do that section; I don't regret that decision, because I was being honest with myself. To compete in any sport, you need to have a well-developed ego. This is especially true before and during an event. You have to tell yourself that you really can do well, and you've got to believe it. At the same time, if things start going wrong, ego can become a big liability unless you know how to adjust. If you've been telling yourself that you're a great athlete, how are you going to feel when you're passed by someone twice your age? Don't think it can't happen, because it *has* happened, even to some top runners. When you just don't have it on a given day, the classy move is to recognize it and give yourself a break. You can learn to enjoy the experience of doing less than well. It doesn't mean you're a "loser," a word that

Left: My maternal grandfather, Leonard Petersen, walked 300 miles from Wisconsin to Chicago after an argument. I inherited his endurance and his sweet tooth—we share a taste for sweet rolls and lemon drops—but fortunately not his temper.

Below: Age 6, a nod to my short-lived ballet career. I was just too hyper for this slow, controlled art form.

Above: During my Negaunee High School years, cheerleading was a huge part of my life. *Top center:* Lori; *middle row, left to right:* Laurie, Kay, Tracy, and Karen (who is now married to my first cousin Marty); *bottom left:* Christine, Steve's sister, who would become my sister-in-law; *bottom right:* me.

Below: Jim and me in downtown Tucson after finishing the Tucson Marathon.

Above: In Surgères, France, with John Geesler, the American record holder in this 48-hour event. We were both dying!

Right: At the Mount Rushmore 100-miler. Jim and all five of our boys came with me to this race. Jim ran with me for the last 10 miles. I took first women's and second overall. The prize was a ring that I haven't taken off since.

Above: Jackson ran with me for the last 4 miles of the 300-mile run. He kept telling me I was going too slow—until I did the last mile in 8 minutes. That shut him up.

Below: My mom caught me at the end of the 300-miler. The hands on the right belong to my friend Tami, a nurse and triathlete who came out to crew. I always collapse like this at the end of a long race—really, it's not as bad as it looks!

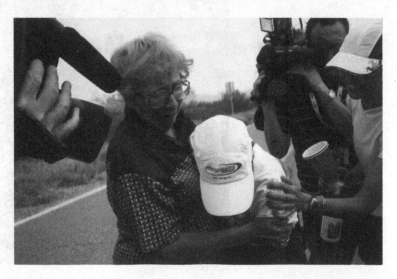

Above: Badwater 2003, the 10:00 a.m. start of the more experienced runners. Many ditched the Lawrence of Arabia head gear; some even exposed their arms and shoulders, which I do *not* recommend. I'm left of the yellow line, wearing my Tucson Marathon T-shirt and my race number, 1, pinned to my shorts.

Right: Coming into Panamint Valley, around mile 60, I was in second place. Once the sun went down I was able to take off my shirt.

Left: At mile 110 of Badwater '03, I passed Chris Bergland to go into first place.

Below: The notorious baby jogger. We actually used this for only about 3 miles, from miles 20 to 23. I was amazed at what a big deal this blew up into in chat rooms and elsewhere!

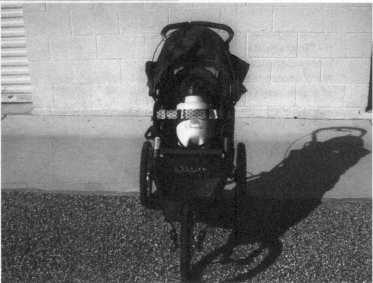

Left: Approaching Lone Pine, around mile 118, about 17 miles from the finish of Badwater '03. As Suzy comes on to pace, Chuck switches off.

Below: Climbing Mount Whitney with my mentor, Benny Linkhart, with Dean Karnazes on my tail. My knee had been killing me most of the way until I tied a sock around it to brace it (a trick I'd learned from runner Paul Schmidt at one of my first 100-milers).

Breaking the tape at Badwater in 2003, I showed that my win the year
before had not been a fluke.

only losers use. I've had bad days and tough races, and I think they've made me a better runner and possibly a better person.

My 2005 experience in the **Grand Teton 100**, near Jackson Hole, will definitely be one of my all-time favorites. Even though conditions were just terrible—cold, snowy, rainy—I was in a good spot mentally. All the obstacles seemed like fun. It's a great feeling when that happens in an ultra event.

In their own ways, the 2005 Leadville and Grand Teton ultras were such intense races that I want to say more about each of them a little later.

Since it's always exciting to be a virgin again, I couldn't resist when my friend Laura Yasso suggested that we run the London and Boston marathons back-to-back in the spring of 2005—a *transatlantic double*. It would have been another first for me, and for Laura, too. I couldn't just stop with that, of course. No. Big-mouth Pam had to say, "You know what would be really cool? We could do the London, fly to Boston, run the Boston back-to-front before the start, and then run the regular race with everyone else! A transatlantic London/double Boston!" What was I, nuts? For sure.

We did it, though, and it was a really neat experience that I doubt I will ever do again! It was a logistical nightmare. We literally had to run from the finish of the London to our hotel just to get to the airport in time for our flight to Boston. The other little matter we failed to take into account was jet lag. I think our times were something like 3:23 (for me) and 4:12 (for Laura) in London; then going "backward" in Boston, we had 4:45 and 5:10, respectively; and going forward, we got 4:18 and 4:50. Don't quote me on those, but I know they were not wonderful times. I don't think I've ever felt so awful—not even after Badwater.

While the transatlantic London/double Boston was an extreme case, in all the 100-plus marathons that I have run, I have always hit the proverbial wall. You might think this wouldn't happen to someone who's used to running much farther than 26 miles, but it does. At least it does to me. There's always a point, at around mile 20, where my legs are just screaming. It's not the lungs; it's the legs. There have been two exceptions. In those cases, I have no idea what, if anything, I did differently. All I know is that I finished those races without experiencing intense pain. Now you'd better believe that I savored that—both the first time and the second!

So, looking for new "virgin territory" to savor is not always about finding something farther or harder, though those things have strong appeal to an athlete of my ilk. Other "firsts" can be very pleasurable, too. And some of them I would never have thought to look for.

Recently, I started doing Pilates. It's totally new and different for me. I taught aerobics for 15 years, but this was something that I couldn't do very well, which is actually a pleasant, exciting feeling: "So, I am going to learn something. Neat!"

Another thing is that I'm now over 45, so I've been thinking about doing Ironman competitions again, though in a different age bracket. I think that will make things interesting.

I've gotten to a point where I feel pretty capable of dealing with physical challenges. It took me a long time, and I'm glad it did. Yet I don't ever want to feel like I've "mastered" this. I don't want to lose the excitement, or even the little bit of fear that comes from going a little farther or trying something new. Lately I've been talking with a few people about doing a 500-miler. Maybe it will be a race; maybe it will be a different kind of experiment and experience—we're playing with several different angles.

CHAPTER 24

FORREST GUMP OF PICACHO PEAK: MY 300-MILER

My reasons for attempting, in March of 2005, to run 300 miles without sleeping have been widely misinterpreted. Locally, the run was very well received—I had tremendous support from the community. And I was told that in various chat rooms and bulletin boards on the Internet, people were following and talking about the effort. My crew, my friends and family, and many people I'd never met before came from all over to help out and lend moral support. In other quarters, I was criticized as a publicity seeker. You can't win.

Even I was conflicted about this event. Dean Karnazes, my fellow ultrarunner, had recently run 262 miles without sleep over a period of 75 hours. He was my inspiration (more on this later). I was not trying to upstage Dean, or trying to challenge him—the challenge we each set for ourselves differed. As impressive as Dean's run was,

I thought that I could go farther. I thought Dean had made a mistake by doing his run in the mountains. I wanted to run 300 miles at one stretch, so someplace reasonably flat made more sense to me.

Picking a date took some planning on Chuck's part. For the sake of convenience, I wanted to do the 300-miler near home. This meant that unless I wanted a superhot run, I needed to do it in either spring or fall. There were other events I wanted to do in the spring. Specifically, I would be doing the transatlantic London/double Boston trip with Laura Yasso. In the fall, I had the Tucson Marathon to see to. So we had to sprint a bit to get the 300 together for Easter weekend, in late March. That date happened to have the added benefit of a full moon, which was due to good luck rather than good planning.

We arranged to do the run on a frontage road that parallels Interstate 10, running between Marana and the Picacho Peak exit. I would cover a 25-mile loop course 12 times without stopping for more than a few minutes. This distance was about 50 percent longer than any single race I'd done before. (My record at that point was 212 miles in 48 hours, in 2004.) Although I was confident that it was doable, I let caution prevail. First and foremost, I'm a mom who has no intention of leaving her sons motherless. Dr. Rich Gerhauser, medical director for the Tucson Marathon, put me through a full battery of tests—bone density, body fat, electrolyte levels, the works. All seemed fine, and I got a green light on the medical front. Still, my son Andrew asked, somewhat tentatively, "There'll be an ambulance there, won't there?" I assured him I'd be fine.

At 6:00 a.m. on March 23, Chuck Giles said, "Go!" And I went, armed with an iPod fully loaded with Andrew's favorite music. I like his taste and trusted him to choose a good soundtrack for my run.

Based on my 48-hour race in which I'd done 212 miles, Chuck was wildly optimistic about how long it would take me to do the run. He thought I could do it in 60 hours—that is, another 88 miles in 12 more hours. I felt that 72 hours was a more reasonable estimate. Even that was very optimistic.

How does someone run 300 miles? Not very fast.

I thought it was pretty incredible that my mom would try to run 300 miles. I thought she was crazy. It was much longer than she'd run before. She wasn't going to stop and she wasn't going to sleep. I wasn't worried, though. I sort of thought she could do it. Well, maybe she could do it.

—*Jackson Reed*

I got a good start on Friday morning, and the first day was very smooth. I was caught up in the excitement of all the supporters around me. There had been a piece in the Tucson paper's sports column about the run, and throughout the day people showed up to watch, crew, or just cheer me on. It was really cool. I had my usual guys there—Chuck, Susy, and Craig, plus my parents. Elisa was there. Tim, Andrew, and Jackson were all there off and on. Jim was busy with taxes again so he couldn't be there. Rich Gerhauser had said he'd be available if we hollered. My friend Linda Brewer, who was covering the run for *Marathon & Beyond* magazine, compiled a list of the professions of everyone who stopped by: "a Presbyterian minister, two nurses, a dermatologist, a carpenter, an English professor, a judge, a medical secretary, a termite expert," and on and on. It was a long list: doctor, lawyer, and Indian chief! A lot of runners showed up to pace me, including an ultrarunner from Brazil; a Moroccan runner who lived in the Tucson area; Dave Hill, who'd won the London Marathon masters class twice; and Jeff Balmat, whom I got to know when he responded to a general e-mail Chuck sent out looking for help with the event (Jeff wasn't a runner before, but he's since become one and done a marathon). People would pull over in their cars, some just getting out to watch and others running along with me for a while.

I was feeling pretty good. Stacy Weisner, who has worked in Chuck's law office for 20 years, sat in an RV at the north end of the loop and counted the laps. When I hit two down, there were only 10 to go.

After sunset, that first 50 miles came back to haunt me. With the various pacers, I'd allowed myself to go too fast. I'd done it in about 8 hours—way too fast for a longer race. It was now cold, and I was afraid that I'd pushed too hard during the day. I was drinking a lot of Ensure, and at around midnight my mom heated up some noodles. Having some food in my stomach helped. Different people were running along with me, handing me applesauce and drinks. I discovered that the road we'd picked for the course was not really ideal after dark. It was hard to tell whether headlights were cars on the frontage road or on the parallel highway. The crew was basically helping me watch out for traffic. My dad, who has always been good at going without sleep, took a shift driving the support van. And a local runner, Bob Wolfe, did the 2:00 a.m. pacing.

In an event like this, the lack of sleep is probably the most difficult part. After years of ultrarunning, my body has adapted to prolonged strenuous activity. Lactic acid doesn't build up in my muscles, and I metabolize nourishment very efficiently. But sleep is something that everybody needs, whether he or she is a runner or not. During sleep, the kidneys stabilize the body's fluid levels. The brain recharges itself. In fact, the brain uses more energy during sleep cycles than when awake. If you don't sleep, you literally go crazy. How long does that take? For some people, a lot less time than I spent on that 25-mile loop. Somehow, miraculously, the lack of sleep didn't really bother me.

The next day, I was happy to get warmed up after that cold night. On Saturday, the temperature got up to around 80 degrees and it felt wonderful. I consciously set my pace slower than the day before. Then, another cold night. This time Tim joined my dad on the night shift. Again my mom was there to feed me noodles. When I was getting ready to do this run, I'd wanted to control everything and make sure that nobody around me would make me feel like quitting for any reason. I'd told my mother that she could only be there for the first 24 hours. After that, I'd said, I didn't want to see her. I'd been so mean! My reason was that she had never seen me during one of my longer races. I was afraid that if I looked bad (which was likely), she'd assume the worst and make me stop. And then I would have had to kill her. Luckily for me, she didn't listen to me—she stayed till the end.

The temperatures that night were in the low 40s. I was feeling pretty cold. Someone brought me a jacket and gloves. I was also having some stomach problems, so I was taking papaya enzyme in a pill form. Chuck had turned me on to this. It really helps to settle your stomach. Bob Wolfe was back at 2:00 a.m., when I was practically asleep on my feet. He'd apparently claimed that shift as his own. I was glad to have his company the next night, too.

Another reliable companion was Pastor John Wall, a member of Elisa's Tuesday morning running group. Pastor Wall had shown up in the wee hours of Friday night and run with me into the dawning Saturday morning. Saturday night he was back again, and we ran together into Sunday. It was like having my own sunrise service for Easter.

• • • • •

I'm sure that after being awake and moving for several days in a row I must have looked pretty awful. At some point, Elisa began to get

concerned about my physical well-being. When we do the Tucson
Marathon, we always have ambulances standing by in case of an
emergency. Despite Andrew's worries, I hadn't thought I'd need
anything like that. Elisa was not so sure, so my mother drove to the
nearest firehouse to inquire about the availability of emergency
medical technicians "just in case." Apparently this created some
drama. It turned out that the nearest firehouse was not in Pinal
County, where I was running. If something had happened, they
would not have been the ones to respond. And when mom found a
firehouse, they told her they didn't know where their ambulances
were stationed. At least that's what she understood. As small as this
place is, they may not even have had their own ambulances, but one
would have been able to respond from nearby Marana. Of course, I
wasn't planning on needing an ambulance. That didn't keep my
mom and Elisa from being pretty freaked out about not having one
available.

With 2 full days of running behind me, the hours crawled by on
Sunday and I was getting more than a little fed up with constantly
consuming fluids. I was drinking tons of Red Bull, Ensure, Amino
Vital, club soda, and frozen Gatorade, as well as grapefruit juice,
Orangina, and an almond-milk drink called horchata. I really
didn't want anything more. But I knew I had to keep drinking,
and if I'd forgotten that, I'd have had plenty of "help"
remembering.

On Sunday evening my friend Paul, whom I know from the
masters swimming program at our local club, visited. Paul had
also stopped by shortly after the start of my run, on Friday
morning, as he and his family were heading off to Flagstaff for
the long holiday weekend. He had wanted to wish me luck with
the run before they left. Now he was back . . . and I was still
running. It was a small thing, but one that gave me a really
interesting perspective on the experience. While I was going

along in my own little universe, the rest of the world was still buzzing along as well.

• • • • •

Even with all my caretakers, after mile 250, I started to feel weak. My legs weren't the problem—they were all right. I just felt down. I had been forgetting to eat, and apparently everyone else had forgotten about feeding me. The run had gone on for so long—we were going into the third night—that even the crew was losing focus. I can't honestly blame them. I think it must have gotten incredibly boring. Staying alert for more than 3 days on the same loop course is really above and beyond the call of duty!

Toward the end, I was doing about 3 miles an hour, roughly an 8-hour marathon pace. The last 25-mile loop took me more than 9 hours, and I had another small food crisis. Somehow I got it into my head that I was "almost finished" and didn't have to eat for the last circuit. In reality, 25 miles is 25 miles. Once more, Ensure and Red Bull came to the rescue.

I might not have been moving very fast, but I was moving. I stopped once for a quick massage when my hip was killing me. Other than that, for the most part, I'd been in motion the whole way, even when eating.

When I got within 4 or 5 miles of finishing, my youngest son, Jackson, came out and ran the rest of the way with me. I actually ran an extra mile—the official distance was 301.08. It had taken me 79 hours and 57 minutes—very far off from my original estimate.

In the end she slowed down. And then, like 2 miles from the end, she really pushed herself.
—*Jackson Reed*

A lot of images from the experience stick in my mind. The glare and the darkness, the heat and the cold, lots of people. For a while there I felt like Tucson's own Forrest Gump. People honked their car horns as they drove by, and someone made a sign that said, "You Go, Girl"—it was close enough to "Run, Forrest, Run" for me!

The weird thing was how good my body felt. I was really amazed. I can remember feeling more beat up after some marathons than I did after running 300 miles.

> She likes to go till she's hurting. I think it's just how her brain functions. [At the finish of the 300], she was pretty much incoherent, really out of it. But it's like she has this strength of mind. Most people would want to pass out. She wants to go do something else. She didn't even know how out of it she was.
>
> **—Tim Koski**

I'd been invited to appear on *The Tony Danza Show* in New York the day after the race. I was determined to get there. Tony's producers had believed in me before I had even proved I could do it—they'd asked me to come on before I had even started the race. Rich Gerhauser and Elisa were worried about my making the trip. They wouldn't let me get onto a plane without a thorough checkup and IV fluids. Rich had told Elisa that if you fly when you are dehydrated, you can get a blood clot. So I was hustled off to Northwest Hospital in Tucson. Everything was fine, except for sore leg muscles and one small blister.

• • • • •

In an interview with various news outlets after the race, I said, "This is the highlight of all the running I've done. This is the hardest run

I've ever done, but it's also the best experience." I still believe that. The 300 was my best experience in terms of the connection I felt with all the runners and others who came out to support me. I'm especially grateful to my family and crew members—the ones who were out there with me for all 3 days and nights, long after the novelty wore off. It took a lot of discipline for the "insiders" to keep it together through the monotonous parts and to keep the energy consistent. Besides the feeding and watering, they had to be my cheerleaders over a really long period of time.

While I was on the course, *60 Minutes* aired the previously taped segment on Badwater. I'm not sure what effect this had on the world as a whole. I assume that for the most part people just thought it was an interesting story and had no awareness of any larger issue surrounding it. In the world of ultrarunning, however, it strengthened the idea of a rivalry between Dean Karnazes and me. Among a group of people who are determined to keep the sport free of hype and grandstanding, such a rivalry was perceived as really bad form. I've tried to make it clear that I agree with them. I don't do what I do to get attention for myself. Nobody loves publicity enough to run for 80 hours without sleep. I will admit that, whenever I'm able to, I do like to land a blow for women, to maybe level the playing field a little.

I can't help but notice that my 300-mile run was almost the exact distance my grandfather covered when he walked from northern Wisconsin to Chicago. So maybe I'm just upholding a family tradition. There's a Finnish word, *sisu*, that means "guts." That's another part of my heritage that I try to live up to.

CHAPTER 25

BADWATER 4:
JOGGER-A-GO-GO

The early summer of 2005 was not one of the high points of my running career. Throughout the spring, I had done a lot of races and runs—the triple marathon (London/double Boston) and the 300-miler at the end of March. Jim said flatly that he thought I was doing too much.

I had set a goal of doing the Western States 100-miler 10 times, and I had run it the 5 previous years, so I wanted to do it in '05 to stay on track. In four of those races I was the 11th woman to finish, and in the fifth I came in 13th. To take part in Western States, you have to not only qualify but also be selected. This year, I barely squeaked in after being told that I didn't have a chance to win. This struck me as a bit harsh since the event has 400 racers each year, and I can't imagine that each and every one is considered likely to win. In the end, I was admitted on a technicality—the volunteers from each aid station along the route are allowed to invite a runner, so I have them to thank for letting me run.

Truthfully, Chuck didn't want me to do Western States either, and maybe he was right. I finished far behind any of my previous results—24 women and numerous men finished before me. I hadn't set any big goals for myself, which was a mistake. Even when you don't set the bar high, you can still be disappointed. Maybe my heart just wasn't in it. After all the drama of getting in, I was thinking of Western States almost purely as a warmup for my fourth Badwater. That's a terrible attitude to have about a 100-mile run, and it's not even how I really feel about this race. I really want to keep on trying it. I feel that I have the ability to do well, though it has never yet come together for me. It's an unusual race because its mixture of high and low elevations causes a lot of variation in the ambient temperature, and a lot of the course is downhill. You might think going downhill wouldn't be that hard, but I can tell you that when it goes on for a while it can be very tough. Your feet tend to land hard, and the pounding has a cumulative effect. It's easy to get injured. I'm not a great downhill runner. Uphill may require more energy and burn more calories, but I do well with that challenge. In fact, as the incline gets steeper, I tend to do better.

Doing well at Western States may very well require not doing Badwater one year, since I tend to hold something back in anticipation of that later race. And that year, the prospect of Badwater was starting to look more like an obligation than an opportunity. I had never felt like that before. Along with that feeling, other new thoughts were coming into my head: If I didn't want to run a 135-mile race across Death Valley, maybe I shouldn't do it. No one was holding a gun to my head. And it wasn't like I hadn't done it already. What was the point?

It took me a while to answer this question. It meant coming to terms with who I am in the world. It may be defensive for me to think of myself as "ordinary." In fact, I'm sure that it is. But that is truly how I think of myself. I very rarely see myself as an athlete, an elite athlete, a world-class athlete. Seeing myself in that role means I have to act the part. It's a responsibility, and it means not paying so much attention to my changing moods and emotions. I'm good at doing this when I'm in a race. As I get older, I have to get good at it off the course as well.

So I decided that I would run in my fourth Badwater after all.

Due to a new regulation that I'll explain in just a second, I had a different crew for the 2005 race. Some of the members were just getting into running, but one had already run a marathon in just over 2½ hours. Equally impressive was that my whole crew had law degrees, doctoral degrees, or medical degrees. If it had been a game of *Jeopardy* instead of a race across Death Valley, we definitely would have won. In many ways it created a very different vibe.

I was hoping for really, really hot weather. The staggered start would begin with the novice runners at 6:00 a.m., another group at 8, and the more experienced people at 10. One of the exciting things about this race was the presence of Scott Jurek, who had just won his seventh Western States. If he was not the favorite to win, it was only because this was his first Badwater. To be honest, I didn't think Scott was going to do that well. He had an amazing record as an ultrarunner, but virtually all of his events had been trail races in relatively cool climates. Badwater would be the first time he was running on scorching hot pavement in temperatures of well over 100 degrees.

As it turned out, the weather was relatively cool—*relative* being the operative word. It never got above 120. Even with such moderate conditions, Scott definitely had some shaky moments toward the end of the desert portion of the race. As night fell, Scott's crew literally submerged him in a vat of ice water.

Nevertheless, he is a phenomenal athlete and was the overall winner, finishing in 24 hours and 30 minutes, a new Badwater record. Very impressive!

My fourth Badwater was not my best or my worst. It didn't have the excitement of the first one, but it wasn't a letdown like the third one, either. The most memorable aspect was an incident that will probably keep all of us either groaning or giggling for years to come.

As I've said, if it were not for Chuck Giles, I don't know whether I ever would have done Badwater in the first place. My doing the race was really his brainchild—he was so knocked out by the craziness of the race that in a sense he was scouting for talent and recruited me to run it. He was the mad mastermind behind me and my crew from the very beginning. Knowing the terrain and being extremely smart, he had figured out how I could best be supported, from what I should eat, to pacing, to keeping me entertained and awake when it was boring and I was tired, to cooling me down. That last point is vital. One thing Chuck always understood about Badwater was the benefit of providing a runner with continuous cooling. To do that, a crew member had to run beside the competitor with a spray bottle. It's not easy to spray someone while you're running, especially for a prolonged period of time. Then Chuck had the idea of putting a crew member on a bicycle. This was a great innovation. It was easy to manipulate the spray bottle while pedaling, and a good cyclist could keep going much longer than anyone on foot. This worked so well for us the first year we competed that a good number of runners in the ensuing years had bicycle escorts. Chuck's insight about continuous cooling dramatically changed Badwater finishing times. The whole tempo of the race picked up.

Despite the benefits to the runners, the crews, and the results, the race organizers were uncomfortable with what was happening. They introduced a no-bicycle rule. This greatly upset our routine because many of our crew members were cyclists first and runners second. That meant that Chuck was going to have to recruit some new faces, or rather legs. We literally needed not just a different crew but a larger crew because runners would tire faster than bikers and need more recovery time between shifts. Chuck on a bike could stay out with me for 4 or 5 hours, but not on foot. So for pacing we continually needed fresh horses, so to speak. Chuck rounded up a crew of amazing runners with great credentials: Susy, Doug Kelly (a friend of Susy's and mine—an astronomer who had run a really fast marathon—2:38—at his hometown Twin Cities Marathon in Minneapolis), and Dave Hill. I'd met Dave when he and his wife, Michelle, showed up at my 300-mile run to run a few miles with me. Dave had twice outright won the Flora London Marathon masters class. Jeff Balmat—the *nicest* guy—who is a Team in Training runner, was also crewing. He ran the 2005 Tucson Marathon in 3:06! The whole crew was selfless.

After rethinking the personnel issue, Chuck still wasn't ready to concede the cooling technology case. The man was born to innovate, so one idea having been shot down was only going to inspire another—necessity is, after all, the mother of invention. He remembered how Marshall Ulrich, on his own, with no crew, had done the Badwater course using a rolling cart he had designed to transport his food and water, and that gave Chuck an idea. He replaced the bicycle with a jogging stroller carrying a spray water jug. The idea was that a crew member could trot beside me while pushing the stroller and keep up an almost constant shower. Chuck carefully checked the rules of the race and found nothing to prohibit this, so the new invention was launched.

As I ran along, my pacer beside me worked the sprayer. It was far from perfect—directing the water with any accuracy turned out to be harder than expected—but I was getting at least *some* of the intended benefits.

We were all quite surprised when the race director, Chris Kostman, pulled up alongside us in his car. He must have been pretty upset because the first words out of his mouth were "That baby jogger's banned. Get it off the course right now."

As I've mentioned, Chuck is an attorney and his reply was to the point. He said, "Show me the rule that says you can't use a baby jogger. There's no such rule."

I didn't stick around to hear how that one turned out. I just kept running. Later I got a blow-by-blow account:

"Well, I don't want people innovating," Kostman said. "I'm the race director and I just banned the jogger. It's an unfair advantage."

Chuck argued that two other teams had more than two vehicles and really big crews. If Chris was concerned about unfair advantages, there was a lot more to think about than someone's baby jogger.

The "no bikes" rule came down 2 months before the race. It was not highlighted in any way; if you thought you already knew the rules and didn't look, you'd have missed it.

I'd had an idea a long time before. And something I had just seen about Marshall Ulrich reminded me of it. He had done Badwaters 3 or 4 years earlier, all by himself, with no crew. I can't remember how long it took him, but it was a long time. He'd invented this very compact cart to transport his food, water, and so forth. So that was the germ of the idea for using the baby jogger to spray water.

At around mile 25, Chris Kostman rolled up beside us with a buddy in his car. He was very agitated. With no greeting, he said, "That baby jogger's banned. Get it off the course right now."

Pam kept running while I had the face-off. I said, "Show
me the rule that says you can't use a baby jogger. It isn't in
there." Kostman said, "I don't want people innovating. I'm
the race director and I just banned it." Right in the middle
of the race. He said, "It's an unfair advantage."

I said, "And 15 crew members and six vehicles—isn't that
also an unfair advantage?" There were two teams that
had that kind of backup—they were able to go on ice
runs, check into a motel for 4 or 5 hours' rest, or whatever
with that many people and cars. Hey, if you don't want
baby joggers, you only need to ban all wheeled
conveyances.

—*Chuck Giles*

This controversy (which later was discussed at length in Internet
chat rooms) was ironic because the jogging stroller had been my
savior and then, in this case, was my demise. I mean, I *love* the baby
jogger. It's the most fabulous invention. It was my babysitter when
my kids were young—I didn't have to leave them with anyone when
I wanted to run. But truthfully, as part of a sprayer, it didn't really
work. The crew couldn't run and squirt at the same time. The water
just went all over the place.

To me, using the stroller didn't matter one way or another.
Getting rid of it meant extra work for the crew, though, who now
had to run and carry the spray jug. And I felt bad for Chuck, who
had really shown some creativity. It all seemed to be making a
mountain out of a molehill. Technically there was no rule against
the jogger. As I see it, the bottom line is that for any event that is
held year after year, people will always dream up new approaches.
They're growing pains.

In any case, my crew totally rocked. Once we couldn't use the wheels anymore, they took turns lugging that big sprayer bottle while they ran the next 100-plus miles.

• • • • •

Although the heat in Death Valley was a bit less intense than during my first Badwater, the temperature in Lone Pine was still well over 100. Because of what had happened the year before, I was really concerned that Monica Scholz was going to sneak up on me again. Several times I asked Susy to drive back to see where Monica was. In reality, Monica was miles behind me. I couldn't seem to get that clear in my mind. Usually I don't pay much attention to the positions of the other runners, but I really didn't want to get passed by Monica again. She's such a great runner in the last stages of a race. No matter how far back she was, I couldn't stop thinking that she might catch me.

Aside from that element of paranoia, I actually was having a fun run. I spent the day tag-teaming with Albert Vallee, who's a really good French runner, and Charlie Engle. I'd known Charlie before, though until a short time before the race I didn't *know* that I knew him. I had read a profile of him in *UltraRunning* magazine and noticed that he was now the producer of the popular television show *Extreme Makeover: Home Edition*. It figured that Charlie was involved with something "extreme." At around this time, I had been having some discussions with a few people about doing some kind of 500-mile event. Although there were no firm plans, the idea seemed to lend itself to some sort of television program; we just weren't sure what sort. So I had searched the Internet for Charlie and was able to make contact. He immediately knew who I was and reminded me that we had run a 24-hour race in San Diego together, as well as another Badwater. Huh. Small world! In any case, once we started talking, we hit it off, and so it was really cool to be running with him on this day.

All day long it was like we were playing a game of tag. Charlie first caught me at around mile 30, and from then on we switched positions off and on, along with Albert Vallee. Scott Jurek was way up ahead, and behind him was the Canadian Ferg Hawke. At one point, I was running along and there was Charlie, sitting in a chair. I passed him. A little later he caught up and passed me. He was having a great day. Finally, at around mile 85 or 90, it was like he said, "See ya later, alligator," and he headed for the finish. In the end, Charlie got third, after Scott and Ferg; Albert took fourth, having passed me around Lone Pine. I took fifth—or first woman, if you want to look at it that way. Despite all of my earlier anxiety, Monica came in 7 hours after me.

At the finish line was the usual small collection of photographers and journalists. Because of the misunderstanding about the spraying machine, I sensed that Chris Kostman was a little less than thrilled when he presented me with my belt buckle. There was a little ceremony with my crew gathered around, and as Chris handed me the buckle, he said, "I'm sure you'll put this in a place of honor in your home," or something like that.

"Well, I've actually got a lot of things like this," I replied—which is true, but it really didn't come out the way I intended. I immediately added, "Of course, nothing means more to me than these belt buckles."

Great. Now *both* feet were in my mouth. I'm sure I sounded less than sincere. It probably didn't help when I said that I wouldn't be attending the party the following evening. To some of the runners, this may have seemed selfish. All I was thinking about was getting back to my family. Although Jim is just as banned from my races as a baby jogger, I do like to see him afterward.

All in all, I don't think I was as gracious as I might have been. In the past, my attitude had always been that the events are about the running. I now realize that if I want to be a role model for the sport, I need to be prepared and positive before and after a race, just as I need to be for the race itself.

There must be a way to respectfully acknowledge your own accomplishments without seeming like a blowhard. I am proud of the fact that, in four Badwater races, I was the overall winner twice and the winning woman three times, and never finished below fifth place. That was difficult for me to accomplish, and I think it will be difficult for anyone else, too. If another woman does it, I look forward to shaking her hand. In fact, I'd even like to be at the postrace party.

CHAPTER 26

LEADVILLE AND
GRAND TETON

I'm not always sure why I decide to compete in a particular event. Sometimes it's just because I want to be out there again. It's a desire that just gets into my head. Other times there's a specific reason, like, for example, it's a race I've never done before or a race that I want to keep doing or do better.

The Leadville Trail 100 takes place in August, about a month after Badwater. I've done this Colorado ultra five times, and my goal is to do it at least 10. There are two difficult things about Leadville. One is the altitude. The course goes along the crest of the Rocky Mountains; the lowest point is 9,200 feet, and the highest is 12,600. The three big climbs have to be done twice because the course is out and back. I've had some good races there and some not so good ones. Once I finished fourth overall, and another time I won my age group. It's not easy. Because of the altitude, a high percentage of starters don't finish the race. I hadn't tried it for a while, so I decided to do it in 2005.

The second difficulty of Leadville is that Jim and I always end up arguing. When I told him I wanted to do the race in 2005, he was not enthusiastic, especially since I needed him to crew for me. Crewing at high altitude is hard work, just as it's hard at the low elevations of Death Valley. At Badwater however, you're working with a bunch of other people on the crew. Crewing Leadville is fairly solitary, so I think a lot of Jim's resistance to it was just anticipation of the boredom.

Despite all of that, he agreed to go with me.

Mile 75 has always been difficult for me at Leadville. It's always something. This time I was doing okay in the race, but I just wasn't feeling well. I was getting slower, and a friend caught up to me. Then she had to walk because she was having some trouble breathing. She suggested that I walk along with her, rather than stop altogether. I hate to walk, but this time I did it anyway. We walked for 7 miles, which was boring and cold. It was after midnight, and any enthusiasm I'd had for the race had pretty much vanished. When my friend felt ready to run again, I said, "You go ahead and I'll catch up with you." Instead I found someone who, like me, had had enough and was getting ready to leave. I asked her for a ride to my hotel. Jim had already gone there a long time before.

In Leadville at one o'clock in the morning, staying in the race might have been easier than quitting. The hotel was closed and locked. A note on the door read, "Please do not ring the bell." Isn't it the guests who are supposed to use "Do Not Disturb" signs? I rang the bell, and the poor guy had to rouse himself. I got some sleep, and in the morning we left for home.

"Well, Mom, how'd you do?" My son Andrew was eager to hear the good news. Well, sorry, Andrew, there wasn't any this time.

"I didn't finish the race, Andrew."

Andrew just looked at me and asked, "Why'd you drop out?"

He wasn't criticizing me, but the question got to me. It struck me that our family has a unique view of the world. If someone runs 80 miles of a 100-mile race up and down a mountain range, what seems incredible to us is not having gone that far, but stopping! Still, I tried to answer Andrew's question: Why hadn't I finished the race?

"I guess I just didn't feel like it."

It was not a very satisfying answer. We would both have to live with it.

It wasn't the first time I had dropped out of a race. Dropping out annoys me, but an annoyance is all it is. I'm not devastated by it. It doesn't cause me to doubt or question myself. In fact, it doesn't cause me to do anything. It happens sometimes that I'm just not into it, and even though I don't like getting a DNF, or "did not finish"—I *hate* to quit—I'm not going to make up an excuse.

A story I once heard kind of reflects how I feel about this kind of experience. In 1957, Willie Shoemaker, who at the time was considered by many to be the greatest jockey in the world, was to ride the favorite, Gallant Man, in the Kentucky Derby. The night before the race, the horse's owner told Shoemaker he'd had a dream about one of his jockeys misjudging the location of the finish line and losing a race. Shoemaker assured him that it wouldn't happen to him.

The next day, however, he did mistake the 16th-mile marker for the finish line and lost the race by a nose.

Needless to say, the horse's owner was quite disappointed. He asked Shoemaker for an explanation.

"Well, I just made a mistake. I blew it."

Later the owner said that if Willie had made any excuses, he might have thrown him out a window. There was no need for an excuse. People make excuses when the reality is something they can't own up to. If you have respect for yourself, the reality is just what is. If I don't do well in a race, I don't make too much of it because it doesn't signify anything to me. It doesn't prove that I'm something different than I thought I was, or something different from the way I've presented myself to other people. It just means I didn't do well in a race, and there's always another race coming up.

As a matter of fact, there was another one just a few weeks after Leadville. It was the Grand Teton 100, not far from Jackson Hole, where our family has a second home. It's a beautiful part of the country that Jim and I both love. As I've mentioned, he'd like us to move there permanently. Jim wanted to run the marathon that runs concurrently with the 100-mile race. As we were getting ready to go, I was talking about how I thought I might fare. I said I felt good about it. My smart-aleck kid, Andrew, referring to Leadville, said very casually, "Well, before you worry about how you'll do, first you'll have to finish."

One thing about the mountains: The weather is absolutely unpredictable. In 5 minutes it can go from sunshine to storm. There can also be a storm at one elevation and completely different conditions above or below. On the day of the race, however, the weather was very consistent. It was just as bad as it could be— everywhere, and for the whole time.

The 2005 Grand Teton 100-Miler was a new event put on by Lisa Smith-Batchen and her husband, Jay, who are accomplished ultrarunners. I admire them not only for stepping up to the plate to put on a race but also for pulling it off despite family complications (of the good sort). They had one adopted child and had been trying to adopt another. Only a week before the race, they got the opportunity to get their second child. They picked up their baby on Monday and then oversaw this 100-mile race on Saturday. I can't imagine taking care of a newborn, with feedings throughout the night, and then pulling off a complicated event like this.

Because this was the first running, only 14 people registered for the 100-mile race. It was pouring rain and freezing cold. The course was a big figure eight, so we were going to pass the starting line twice. With a wind so strong that it knocked over the aid station tents at the higher elevations, Lisa and Jay had to change the layout of the course after the race started. Visibility was so poor that I could hardly see anything. I'm not even really sure what the course turned out to be. I just followed directions as they were given.

Jim managed to do the marathon—it took him 8 hours in that crappy weather—and then he left the course.

I kept running. I ran for 28 hours in ice-cold mud. Just like with any long race, there was lots of time to think. Many of my thoughts were about the nice, warm motel. I was freezing and so uncomfortable. At one point I started thinking of Jim and made myself mad by thinking that he was all snug and warm while I was out there running. I noticed yet another reason why it's not good to have Jim go with me to races.

If I see Jim during a race, I know that he can take me away from the pain. Had he driven up that night when I was running at Teton, I would've gotten in the car. I'm kidding, but it's also true. It's not just that I want to quit if he's mad at me for not trying hard enough. I'd also want to quit if he babied me.

This was an interesting realization. Now when it's the middle of the night during a long race, I still get a little mad, thinking, "Where is he? He's probably sleeping! He doesn't even care about me if he's sleeping while I'm out here killing myself." Then the next minute I'm thinking, "No, if he's sleeping, that's because he *does* care about me. He doesn't want me to quit because he knows I hate quitting."

At Teton, really, in spite of how bad it was, it was also incredibly exhilarating. There was not a moment when I honestly thought about not finishing the race. The whole race was a blast. I was really in a zone the whole time, feeling almost giddy. I kept thinking how different from Badwater this race was—one hot and dry, the other cold and wet. It made me high to think, "Wow, I can do both kinds of races." I certainly didn't feel tired. How mysterious!

In any sport—though I think especially in running—it seems that there are three different kinds of athletes who can produce really outstanding performances. The first is someone who simply has superior physical gifts. These people are rare, but you know one when you see one. They seem like they're from another planet. Although I don't follow boxing closely, even I was aware of a period when it seemed that Mike Tyson had won dozens of fights by a knockout in the first round. It was impossible to imagine who could ever beat him.

That's the thing about physically superior athletes. It's impossible to imagine them losing until they lose—and sooner or later they always do. In fact, superior athletes can be undone by their very superiority. They're used to winning easily. Their physical gifts are so well developed that their determination has never had to develop correspondingly. If you can make them stretch past their comfort zone, they often fold. Until that happens, these are the people who set the records and write sports history.

The second kind of athlete also has real physical gifts, but not quite at the level of Superman or Wonder Woman. Athletes in the first category win big, except for the few times when they fold. Those in the second category do not always win; they *are* always close. They are always "in the money" and they almost never collapse.

Athletes in the third category are interesting. These people don't have to be especially gifted. Physically they may be only average. But they tend to be resilient, and on a given day, for some mysterious reason, they are able to come up with a performance that's much better than anything they've done in the past. It's like some extra spirit takes hold for a short time and transforms them into stronger and faster competitors.

Of these three categories, I consider myself to be in the second—and now and then in the third. The Grand Teton race in 2005 was one of those unusual occasions. It was amazing to experience the freezing mud almost as a source of pleasure, and doubly so because I really, really hate the cold.

Jim was totally shocked that I completed the 100 miles, partly because this race turned out to be so much tougher than Leadville. I really had a great time! Of the 14 competitors, there were 11 finishers, which is a very high percentage given the kind of race it was. I think Lisa and Jay extended the allowable time by a couple of hours in recognition of how difficult it was. I finished first among women and third overall. I had been ahead for much of the race, but toward the end I was just so tired. I was going a lot slower—I went "bonkola," and a couple of guys got by me.

Those two events—Leadville and Teton—were two sides of the same coin: In one, I gave an uncharacteristically disappointing performance when I really could have finished, and in the other I did much better than I might have considering the far worse circumstances. If I hadn't known it before, I definitely know now that, at the elite level, the mental and emotional elements of running are by far the most important. I'd love to be able to plug into the mind-set I had at Grand Teton. I want to try to make that happen intentionally, instead of having it be a pleasant surprise. I'm confident I'll be able to do that. I had a chance to give it a try at the San Diego One-Day Race a short time later.

CHAPTER 27

ONE DAY
IN SAN DIEGO

Every running event is competitive, but usually I feel like I'm competing against myself. Most of the time I try not to think about the other runners—who's ahead of me or who's coming up from behind—because it can affect my performance. I just focus on being consistent, on keeping myself fed and hydrated, and on getting through the pain that's sure to arise sooner or later. So one event that I ran in the fall of 2005 was a different kind of experience for me. I had to think about actually "beating" other runners.

I was also more aware of the fact that on any given day, one person's head is going to be in a better competitive frame than another's. Just before heading to California for the San Diego One-Day Race, I'd run into a significant glitch with organizing the Tucson Marathon, which was just a few weeks away. For the first time ever, we'd had our course approved before the very last minute. So naturally, this year our finishing area was in dispute. Finishers would have to finish in the parking lot at the end of the race, as they had done in years past. This year the owner of the lot voiced concern about possible accidents—runners tripping over curbs or something. I told him we had insurance; he said that he did, too, but that his lawyer still felt it wasn't worth the risk. We'd have to change the course to have it end somewhere else. This was eventually straightened out when the police of Oro Valley, the Tucson suburb in which the marathon ends, went around and assured the property owners that everything would be seen to in the safest possible way. Along with all the other last-minute details of the marathon, this episode was definitely an added stressor, something I had to forcibly "shake off" before my San Diego start.

The San Diego One-Day Race is an annual event that is open to anyone. That year an invited American team was to compete for the men's and women's American National 24-Hour Run Championship. I was named to the team, so I would try to be the American woman to run the farthest in 24 hours. The organizers had also invited Japan to field a team of their top runners, making this the first international dual meet at the One-Day race. Japan is very strong in the 24-hour event. Their team included the 2004 World 24-Hour Run champions as well as the all-time Asian 24-hour record holders, Ryoichi Sekiya and Sumie Inagaki. Going into the race, Sekiya and Inagaki were the "overwhelming favorites," as it was put in a *Cool Running* article.

On the American team we had John Geesler, who had been the top U.S. finisher in every year that the 24-hour international race had been held. His personal record (PR) for this race was 157 miles, versus Sekiya's PR of 167.3 miles. Among the American women considered potential winners or placers were Stephanie Ehret, Rebecca Johnson, and me. In 2004, Rebecca had won this event, which was held a week after I returned from running in the Czech Republic, and I dropped out after 80 miles. Both Stephanie and I had been top U.S. women placers at the world event. Stephanie had placed third in the world championship in the Czech Republic in 2004; my best showing was sixth that same year. We also had Sue Ellen Trapp, who holds the record for the U.S. women's 24-hour run: 145.2 miles. She had not been racing for a while due to an injury. Now she was back, at the age of 59. Our main competition from Japan, Sumie Inagaki, had in the previous two international competitions taken first and third—she was truly a force to be reckoned with. My main concern was to recapture the U.S. women's title, which I'd won in 2003 by running 138.9 miles. To a great degree, therefore, I was more focused on my American competitors.

The location was Hospitality Point in Mission Bay, near San Diego. That sounds lovely, doesn't it? Parts of Mission Bay are really gorgeous. Unfortunately, this particular area, which we'd spend a lot of time looking at before darkness fell, is not especially scenic. The course was a long, narrow east-west rectangle with the start and finish at the northwest corner—a parking lot. About 100 runners, all wearing electronic ankle bracelets that recorded each lap of the 1-mile loop course, would start together at 10 o'clock on a Saturday morning. Running south for a short stretch, we'd get a view of the Mission Bay channel before turning east onto the south side of the loop—Jetty Road, asphalt with scrubby weeds alongside. Then there was a short bit of dirt path northward before heading west along the longer north side of the loop, Quivira Boulevard. Unlike in races held on an actual track, in this event we ran in the same direction for the entire 24 hours. This, combined with the dirt stretch that was uneven compared to the road, really killed the feet.

I was hoping to complete at least 140 laps. I was also hoping to be the winning woman, and certainly the winning American woman.

Although I was part of the American team, this race was really an individual competition. With everyone pressed together on the same 1-mile course, there was no way to forget about other runners, as I like to do in point-to-point events. Here there were people ahead of, beside, and behind me. Needless to say, this can become confusing. At any point, I might have several times lapped a runner who was physically in front of me, so he or she was actually far behind me in the standings. And someone who was running behind me could actually be ahead of me. After 12 to 14 hours of running around a rectangle, all of this can really start to blur. You have to keep tabs objectively by having a helper check your status and that of your main competitors. For this reason, Susy had come to California with me for the race.

Right from the beginning there was a competitive feeling about this event. At the start of most ultra races there's a kind of celebratory atmosphere. People are pumped up to an almost sickening degree, whooping and hollering. They know it's going to be hard, and they want it to be fun, too. As I watch them, I think about how, in a couple of hours, they'll be getting really quiet. The hoopla wears off pretty fast. I want to tell them, "Don't waste your energy—you're gonna *need* it." Some of the runners who had signed up for this race must have been approaching it with that same sense of bravado. The members of the invited teams were all elite runners, which gave everything an overall intensity.

Going in, my plan was to get two laps ahead of the other women as quickly as I could. Then I would try to maintain that lead. If I couldn't maintain it, I would at least have a cushion that the other runners would have to overcome. I planned to do steady 10-minute miles for as long as I was able to sustain that pace.

It didn't go exactly as I had intended. A young woman whom I didn't know seemed to be running very fast and strong. She was completely messing up my plan of getting ahead and then holding a steady pace. In order to do that, I had to get out in front, and that wasn't happening. It was making me nervous. I had to find out who this woman was, so I picked up my pace until I was running fast along with her. I started making "casual" conversation. I learned that her name was Carol O'Hear and she was 30 years old. I asked if she ran a lot of 100s. She had done some, including Western States, where she'd been the third women's finisher. I was trying to gauge whether she was likely to blow up or whether she could keep this pace going. She certainly wasn't a novice. Still, I was pretty sure that running for 24 hours was new to her. At any rate, I was certain she couldn't keep up an 8-minute pace or anything close to it for very long. So I was able to relax somewhat and get back to running my own race. As it turned out, Carol opened up a big lead, then ran out of gas about 8 hours in.

Again, worrying about other runners was a strategy that I don't often get into. All ultra events are hard, and the competition in this one made it hard in a different way. I'd had a plan, but I'd had to make adjustments. And the race was far from over.

The day had been sunny and hot, but as soon as the sun went down, it was cold and clammy by the bay. Susy had gotten badly sunburned, which of course made her feel even colder during the night. Since she wasn't running, I knew she was freezing. In spite of her discomfort, she did a great job of keeping me fueled, handing me mashed potatoes and oatmeal so I wouldn't have to stop to eat. Other than bathroom breaks, I stopped only twice during the whole race, both times to get a quick massage from a friend of one of the other runners. I stopped for $1\frac{1}{2}$ minutes the first time and 2 minutes the second.

To a minimal degree, I kept tabs on the women's favorite, Sumie Inagaki. There was a board that indicated each runner's number of completed laps, and I'd asked Susy to check it for me because I couldn't see it without stopping. I'd really been most focused on my challenger for the top American woman spot, Rebecca Johnson. Technically, I suppose I was *her* challenger since she'd won this race the year before. She is a fierce competitor. I had no illusions that she'd simply break at some point. She was *that* good.

I tried to break her at hour 12. She just didn't seem to want to get with my program. I mean, come on, Rebecca, couldn't you take a hint? No, she couldn't. Of course, it was mutual. We were really trying to blow each other out. I could literally feel her willpower. Together we did a full lap at a 7-minute pace. This is something I'll have nightmares about for a long time. Running at an amazing pace and not getting ahead was a truly surreal experience. It was also not what I wanted to do by any means. I decided to slow down. I still kept her in range—I couldn't afford to let her get a huge lead. For hours 16, 17, and 18, I just hung with her. Finally, at around hour 19, I began to get an inkling that she might have a breaking point.

She and I were right beside each other, but she was actually two laps ahead. Still, I could see that she was starting to fall apart. I'd noticed that she wasn't eating, and I could tell she was in pain. When hour 20 came, I went as hard as I could. I passed Rebecca after two laps, then passed her again. After 22 hours, I was three laps ahead of her. I did 8:20s for about an hour and 45 minutes until I just conked. My wheels totally came off. But it was enough. Another tactical decision had paid off. The race was almost over.

The event seemed to be turning out well for me. Stephanie Ehret had been running with her husband, Peter Bakwin, and while she had looked really strong, Peter seemed to be having a bad day. They decided to drop out when they reached 100 miles. I believe Stephanie might have done much more. Sometimes your energy level gets linked to the people around you. It's amazing how sensitive you can become during a long race. Your emotional insulation just evaporates.

As time ran out I became more aware of Sumie Inagaki. Because of my concerns about Rebecca, who had been winning overall, I hadn't been as focused on Sumie. Even though all the Japanese runners were really friendly, there wasn't too much American interaction with them since they didn't speak English. I had heard someone say that Sumie had passed Rebecca. Since I had lapped Rebecca, I hadn't thought that much about it. When Susy checked Sumie's mileage for me, she discovered that Sumie was ahead by 1 mile!

I don't know if I could have caught her—the duel with Rebecca had taken so much out of me. In any case, nature was calling urgently, so I had to take an inopportune break. If I'd thought we were even, I would have tried to hold it and stay with her. As it was, she beat me by 2 miles. I finished with 134.433 miles. Sumie took the overall women's title, and Rebecca finished as the second American woman, with 130.913 miles.

Among the men, the Japanese threat, Ryoichi Sekiya, had only managed 10th overall. I'd actually beaten him, coming in seventh overall. American men took all three top spots—Steve Peterson was first; Roy Pirrung, who at age 57 was still finishing near the top in any competition he entered, was second; and Alex Swenson was third.

All in all, it was a great race for me. I was happy with the decisions I'd made. Toward the end, it really seemed like I had outsmarted everybody, which was fun. When I discovered that I wasn't as smart as I thought—that Sumie had gotten by me—that was a good lesson to learn.

My most recent race always seems like the hardest. However, this truly was the most competitive and concentrated event I've ever done. There were several times when I felt myself mentally dropping out and began to give myself permission to do that. When I saw Stephanie Ehret leave, the temptation was even greater. Running for 24 hours is hard enough; *competing* the whole time is really exhausting. I have never before experienced head-on competition like I had with Rebecca Johnson that day—we really killed each other.

[THREE]

WHERE I'M GOING

CHAPTER 28

GOALS

I n my experience, it's never a good idea to go into an event with the sole idea that you are going to win. I'm not saying that I never do this. I'm saying that the result of my doing this is rarely that I achieve that goal. Sometimes the result is worse than if I had not had that goal at all. I put so much pressure on myself that if I don't have a really great start, I can lose sight of the longer race. Someone passing me can be defeating because I am so set on being first that every single thing takes on too much importance. Then my head has more ways to mess with me.

An example of this was one of the times I ran the Leadville 100. A lot of this race is at high altitude, and I'm prone to altitude sickness, which makes me vomit. This in itself isn't that big of a deal. Lots of people throw up during ultra races. It's just one of those things. You throw up, then you get moving again. It's a long race, and you can always regain lost ground. But because I'd had *winning* the race as my only goal going in, when I had to stop to throw up and people began to pass me, it seemed that I'd never be able to do what I'd come to do. So I cashed it in.

What works best for me is having at least three goals and then being flexible even about those. Training and experience can make you more ready and more likely to do better on any given day, but there will always be that occasion when, no matter how prepared you are, it just isn't your day. For me, when that happens, more often than not it's a mental thing. Sometimes I'm able to override it and accomplish at least one of my goals. Sometimes, if I take a long view of the situation, I just decide it isn't worth it. And other times— though rarely—there is a physical reason to quit. I never want to injure myself so badly that I can't come back another day.

Nevertheless, the first goal I start out with is simply to finish. In the kinds of races I run, this is not a small goal; it's certainly not a given. Badwater is an exception in that it gives runners a pretty big window of time to finish the race. In most 100-milers, the time allowed is short enough that frequently half or more of the runners *don't* finish. Finishing requires tremendous effort—often an all-day effort, or longer. Still, given my level of training, I do feel that this goal, for me, is nearly always attainable.

Once the mental box for finishing is checked, my second goal is to make the race a personal best. I like to see whether I can beat the best time I've ever had in a particular event. I can also try to improve my time for just a particular stretch of a long race. Maybe overall I won't have the best time ever—maybe it's not even close. But if I knock 10 minutes off my best time up an 18-mile hill, I still feel a sense of accomplishment.

The last of the three goals is actually winning the race. While I put it last, the reality is that of course this goal is there right from the start—just not to the exclusion of the other two. Since I do some of the same races over and over, the irony is that I could actually achieve this goal without achieving my second goal of a new PR. Sometimes—though not often—running the race in a time that's less than my PR is enough to win.

I want to say one thing in conclusion about the dreaded DNF, which stands for "did not finish." While a lot is made of the notion that finishing is the *least* you can do to keep your integrity intact, that's not true. Killing yourself for a sporting event is just stupid. Ultra events of all kinds—running, biking, or Ironman—take strength, stamina, guts, and maybe just a *little* insanity. Most people wouldn't even attempt these kinds of races. The way I see it, if your mind is urging you to drop out of the race and the race is one that's important to your career or even just to you personally, try your best to overcome it. There are so many things that can affect you mentally—stuff with family or work, or simple boredom. Some days you get into the pool and just swim and swim and everything feels good, and some days you think about every stroke. In a long race there are always peaks and valleys. If you're not into it, just keep going and chances are that the low feeling will pass.

On the other hand, if your body is urging you to quit—not over just a cramp or a blister or fatigue but over something more serious—let your body win. What's the point of finishing a 500-mile bike race if it cripples you so badly that you can never bike again? Even in extreme racing it's important to keep a perspective on how extreme is too extreme.

CHAPTER 29

DESPERATE
HOUSEWIFE?

For the most part my experiences with journalists and the media have been pretty positive. Not surprisingly, a lot of people who write about running are runners themselves, though not professionals. I guess that's because running is something pretty much anyone can do—whereas I'm sure it's less likely that everyone who writes about professional football or even swimming feels like that sport is something they, too, could be good at. Because distance running usually is not done in a confined space like a field or court or arena, a journalist writing about what I do frequently will go for a run with me. So we establish a kind of camaraderie that we wouldn't get if we were doing an interview while sitting across a table from each other. Under the circumstances, I usually feel pretty relaxed and talk about whatever is on my mind and joke around or whatever.

I'm not a celebrity. Even in the world of sports, I'm not nearly as well known as the stars of professional baseball, tennis, or golf. Even though there have been feature articles on me in various publications and I've been on TV talk shows and even in a piece on *60 Minutes*, I'm still a little surprised when someone comes up to me in a store or airport and says, "Hey, aren't you Pam Reed?" When I'm interviewed for TV shows or news articles, I don't always have a prepackaged sound bite prepared, though maybe I should. I haven't given a lot of thought to "controlling my image." It's just not something I dwell on. I'm more likely to just say the first thing that comes into my head.

Occasionally, this lack of awareness has come back to bite me. There definitely have been times when I've thought I was just chatting, but the interviewer apparently has had another agenda besides just seeing what I'm up to and what I might be doing next. This is a lesson that was brought home to me very clearly when a journalist asked if she could observe the 300-mile run I did in March 2005 and spend time with me several times after that for a feature piece in an outdoors magazine.

The way it was presented to me was that she wanted to write an article that would examine the difficulties of being a woman athlete, how tough it was to be a full-time mom and still train and compete, and so on. Since this is a subject that is really important to me, I was happy to talk with her. I thought that it might result in an important story that could be helpful in some way to other women. The journalist was really friendly and encouraging. How wonderful! She ended up being with me for all 4 days of my 300-mile run, visiting with me at my home in Tucson, and accompanying me to Lake Tahoe for the 100-mile Western States, where I spent a couple of hours with her before and after the race. A photographer accompanied her. Rolls and rolls of film were shot throughout this process—hundreds of pictures of me.

I took this situation at face value. I felt comfortable with the journalist and for the most part enjoyed her company, even though there were definitely other things I could have been doing with my time.

Then the article was published in the October issue of the magazine.

Let me start by saying this: I'm used to the "Are you crazy or just nuts?" kind of questions. That's the easy way to open a discussion of any extreme sport, from ultrarunning to everything from snowboarding to NASCAR racing. The writer usually gets that out of the way and then gets down to the business of what the article is really about—some aspect of the sport or the person or the event. This was the first time I've ever been the subject of a piece where, upon reading the result, it seemed to me that the sole purpose for profiling me had been to set me up as a crazy person.

Although I don't remember exactly, it's possible that the quotes in the article are things I had actually said. I'm hugely outspoken, so maybe I have to learn not to say everything there is to say without thinking about how it can be slanted to change what I actually meant. Even though much of my conversation with the journalist had a kidding tone, remarks I'd meant in a humorous way were presented in the article as being completely serious as well as indicative of my true character.

And then there were the photos. Hundreds of photos were taken. They printed one of me in my sauna that caught me transitioning between expressions and blew it up to fill a full page. Are you telling me that this was the best one they got? No. I feel that they intentionally picked one that they thought made me look crazy. And this was their storyline: I was a crazy "desperate housewife" stalking another (male) athlete who was presented as some kind of matinee-idol pretty boy—Dean Karnazes. Supposedly, since Dean had beaten me at Badwater the previous July, I was obsessed with him, jealous of his fame, and so on.

When I read the story, I felt that the whole time we were hanging out together, this writer must have known that she wanted to construct a feud between Dean and me that didn't even exist. She was just looking for a nugget here and a nugget there that she could bend to fit her concept.

According to the article, I was bitter because Dean had gotten a lot of press and I had gotten less, even though I had finished ahead of him in the 2003 Badwater race. I was supposed to have become even more bitter when he won the following year.

In all honesty, I don't care about the personal stuff. I've got a thick skin—thick as a "desert tortoise" or "a hide," according to this article. What a zinger! I simply don't see how it benefits my sport to hold up to ridicule a top female athlete—or male athlete for that matter, because I don't think Dean could have appreciated being presented as having most of his talent in his face or his marketing savvy. I wish—not for my own sake but for the sake of ultrarunning—that the long-term good of the sport had not been sacrificed for short-term sensationalism and negativity. It's been hard enough to establish and legitimize ultra events in people's minds.

Since the piece appeared in a national magazine and contained numerous misconceptions, I would like to take on a few of the issues that I think were misrepresented.

First, the subject of "fame" and my supposed craving for it: Well, that's not exactly how I see it. I don't think, "Someone else is famous so *I* want to be famous." It's about due recognition. And I do think this is important. It is true that I complained (I've said before that I am a world-class complainer) about the fact that after he won Badwater in 2004, Dean's picture was on the cover of *Runner's World* magazine. My point wasn't anything against Dean. It was that since, generally speaking, it is expected that Badwater will be won by a man—until my 2002 win, it had never been won by a woman—the media should have treated the first female victory as a bigger deal. Then, for a woman to defend that win, winning 2 years in a row—

you'd think that someone might have found that worthy of more than a passing comment. There were articles about it, but the coverage was not spectacular. The following year, it was back to business as usual: A man won. Now this was *big* news. Picture-on-the-cover news. I think it sent a general message to women that we are not newsworthy, no matter how laudable our accomplishments. I perceive an obvious double standard. The outdoors magazine article about Dean and I did include a comment that I made about women needing their due recognition. The article's overall tone of ridicule—of both me and Dean—overshadowed anything positive they said about the sport or anything serious they said about women.

Second, with regard to my 300-mile run supposedly being my way of stalking Dean, the truth is that any runner of long distances always has simmering on his or her back burner that one run they'd eventually like to do. Granted, I can't pretend that a 300-miler had been on my to-do-someday list. The decision came about more like this: As I've already mentioned, my complaint about Dean's *Runner's World* cover was that a man winning the race got more publicity than the much less common occurrence of a woman winning the race. I was going on and on about this at the time, and I think I must have gotten on my husband's last nerve with it. In the *Runner's World* article, Dean had said that he would like to be the first person to run 300 miles nonstop. So finally—maybe just to shut me up, but also, I like to think, because he does have a lot of faith in my capabilities—Jim said to me, "Do you think you could do that?" The question just hung there for a few beats, and then I said, "Let me think about it." And I did. For the next few days, I really thought about it. And then I said to Jim, "Yes, I can do that." And we began to plan for it. So, although I'm proud of having done the run, I have to give credit where credit is due: The so-called "stalking" was not stalking at all; it was Jim's idea, and it really began as a simple question that arose from Jim's loyalty to me.

A third contention in the article was that I was supposedly obsessed with money, or, rather, sponsorships. The whole idea that it's somehow delusional or a character flaw to want to earn money for competing as a professional in a sport is, to me, ridiculous.

I've done my best to develop myself as a runner. To do that, I've had to put out, year after year, a very healthy chunk of change. Participating in sports is expensive. A pair of running shoes costs $100 or more. Travel, hotels, and meals when I'm competing away from home (I run an average of 24 events per year, all over the country and internationally)—they all take money. Then there's medical attention and ground transportation during long races. I have to forget about paying my crew—they do an event as a huge, amazing gift to me. I can't put them on my payroll, but nobody deserves it more.

Since this seems to be such a novel concept for at least some journalists who have written about me, it should be noted that most ultra races involve no purse whatsoever. The big, bad Badwater belt buckle—what you get for running the most grueling race of all—has become almost legendary as a symbol of "why bother?" I really don't see anything wrong with a corporate entity supporting me so that I can provide them with publicity that amounts to product placement. If Ford is willing to provide vehicles for the transportation of my crew on long races, I'm delighted. If Red Bull or Recover-Ease wants runners to know that their products are serious fuel for endurance sports, or if my wearing PowerSox shows other runners that this is a reliable product, it is a mutually beneficial arrangement. I make no apologies. Think about it: Women are the main purchasers of all these products, both for themselves and for their families.

And here's how these three things tie together: Even though running 300 miles was Dean's goal originally, my 300-miler was not about Pam versus Dean, but about what women are accomplishing in sports. It may be difficult for some guys to understand that an athlete would identify with her gender to such a degree that she would even put it before personal recognition. Women have had to fight and fight and fight some more to be (a) permitted to play, (b) funded to play because playing costs money, and (c) recognized for playing well because it is this recognition that then attracts money (see b) that facilitates being able to play (see a).

Whew! It's enough to make a housewife desperate.

CHAPTER 30

FRIENDS AND FAMILY

When I was growing up in the UP of Michigan, my family did lots of things together. Besides the trips to Beaver Lake and other destinations for skiing or snowmobiling, we also took some memorable vacations—we visited a number of European countries and Hawaii. There were also car trips exploring the Western states. This was back before seat belt laws, and I have vivid memories of making forts in the back of the car with my sister, Debbie. We carried on back there, missing much of the scenic landscape we passed through. I now have a greater appreciation for beautiful surroundings than I did as a kid.

We were not the Cleaver family. I recall sitting in restaurants, my sister and I blowing the paper covers off our straws at each other while my mom egged us on, much to my poor father's embarrassment. There was also a fair amount of "frank discussion" in our home. I could also put it this way: Voices were often raised, and there were arguments about lots of different things. Debbie and I squabbled a good bit just because we were different types of girls. She was more girlish and I had tomboy tendencies; she liked things to be neat and the games I enjoyed tended to mess things up. I'd get into her things, she'd scream at me, and I'd scream right back.

Despite our differences, I was closer to my family than to anyone else back then. Like any normal kid, I had some good friends in the neighborhood and at school. But even in high school and college I never really had a friend who changed my life. I had close friends, but we didn't keep in touch after graduation. My father, my mother, and my sister were the center of my emotional universe. This was true until I moved away and had children of my own.

It's kind of funny that I came from a family of all girls except for my father and now I'm in a family of all boys except for me. I believe in God, and I believe that He arranged this for me. As much as I want that proverbial level playing field for women in sports and everywhere else, I can't imagine myself having girls. My mothering style is a bit rough—I can be way bossy—and sometimes even my sons get mad at me. One reason I have never coached is that I'm afraid I might be too mean. I think I missed sensitivity training. I just hope the boys know that I really do love them. With Jim's sons, Jonathan and Greg, I'm pretty hands-off. I'm the stepmom and they have their mother, so I don't feel that it's my place to tell them what to do. They're mostly shielded from my bossiness.

I don't know whether Jim and I set the best example with regard to relating to each other. I may have mentioned once or twice that our m.o. can be combative. Jim has watched all of the *Godfather* movies—*all* of them—about 20 times. He *loves* the *Godfather* movies. He is a regular Vito Corleone when it comes to family. It's the godfather code of ethics: "If you mess with my family, you're messing with *me*." That's really neat, but you can take it too far.

My oldest, Tim, and I have a weird, almost brother-sister–type relationship. He yells at me and calls me on my behavior and my views. He thinks of himself as the sane, sensible one. And he actually is. I've never forced my kids to run, but I do get on their case if they're shirking activities or sports they signed up for at school. One day when Jackson didn't want to go to his tennis lesson, I said, with a great deal of force, "*You gotta go to tennis!*" This prompted Tim to say, "You see? *That's* why I didn't want to go to practice."

One way that Tim—and Jackson also—is like me is that we are not good at taking compliments. We feel funny about it. If I tell Tim, "Good job," he totally blows it off. He has played baseball since he was 5, and if he hits a home run it's like, "Whatever." He doesn't want people to think he's doing anything to impress anyone. When Jackson is playing soccer and does well, he deflects any praise he's given. Maybe he will grow out of this.

Andrew, my middle son, is different—he likes to be acknowledged. He's more social in a way, a people pleaser. He likes praise, and he does better when people have a positive attitude toward him. I have to be careful because he gets upset if I get mean or aggressive with him. The way I think he and I are most alike is in our spontaneity. He's very off-the-cuff; he seems to do things without thinking about them too much. That's not always a good thing. Recently, for some reason he smashed a bunch of mailboxes in the neighborhood. I really gave him hell for that.

My kids are not angels, and they should know that when they mess up, they won't get away with it. Andrew and Tim have this in common with their dad. They usually are really good kids, and when they aren't, they get caught. They are just not good at being sneaky. A couple of years ago Tim and a few friends tried to get into a Native American casino using fake IDs. Just like his dad when he tried to cut school, he was found out. Maybe I don't catch the boys personally, but God is watching!

On the other hand, sometimes my sons make me so proud. In high school, Tim's baseball workouts got more intense; the coach had them doing 6-minute miles. I'd tell him, "That's amazing; that's great." He hated it, though. He would get almost physically sick at the thought of running. Then, 2 years ago, he ran the last 10 miles of Western States to pace me. He helped me finish in under 24 hours. That was really one of my proudest moments! Now Tim runs for fitness and aspires to do a marathon.

Andrew is a great kid with a very funny, nonchalant way of talking to me, very deadpan. He was with me when I was doing the 48-hour race, and at one point I was really losing it. I said, "Andrew, I'm *dying! What am I gonna do?*" And he said, "You know, Mom, if you just hold on and do what you always do, you'll be fine." I just kept that in my head, and he was right.

My family has taught me some lessons about prioritizing my athletic activities versus my mom duties. One particular race comes to mind. A couple of years ago when I was scheduled to do the Old Pueblo 50-Miler, Jackson was pretty sick. Although I was worried about leaving him, I was stuck in the groove that says, "You signed up for this race; you have to follow through." As I traveled all the way to the race and with every step I ran, the thought kept nagging at me that maybe I shouldn't be doing it. Finally, about halfway through the race, the realization broke through my hard head: "What on earth are you doing out here? You have a sick child at home!" I dropped out and went back to my kid. It was like a lightbulb had gone off. Not only is it okay to put being a mom first sometimes, it's the right thing to do.

I feel very lucky to have my family, and I'm also very lucky to have my friends. Right now, I have more close friends than I did earlier in my life. I see some of them almost every day. My closest friends are also my running partners. Since I run every day, we have really gotten to know each other.

In fact I think, especially in recent years, running has helped a lot of women to develop close friendships with other women. On my runs, I often see other women running in groups of two or three. Though this may be different in other parts of the country, for some reason I rarely see groups of men. Is it because women are more likely to either work at home or have flexible work schedules? Maybe—but I also think it's because running is more and more becoming a female activity. In the Tucson Marathon, for instance, the number of women runners has been going up. For the past 2 years there have been more women than men registered for the race.

My closest running girlfriends in Tucson are Susy, Rhina Gerhauser, and my Tucson Marathon sidekick, Elisa Kinder. In Wyoming, my most frequent running partner is my friend Patty Gill, whom I consider the mom of the century, with three boys and two girls. My friends are all good runners, even if they're not in the elite category at the moment. Outside of running, their lives are all different, which always makes for an interesting conversation.

Elisa and I usually run our dogs together. We talk about the marathon or another subject that comes up a lot, diet—not for weight loss, but for nutrition and health. Elisa had a problem with rheumatoid arthritis in her hands—thankfully, it's in remission now, through a lot of hard work and a special diet. Even though she put up with a lot of pain, it didn't seem to affect her running. Her father was a doctor—in fact, he was Fidel Castro's personal physician before emigrating to this country and joining the Army—and I think Elisa inherited a "doctor" gene from him. She is always telling me what I should eat for this or that, or telling me what she is eating for some health issue or another. She knows a lot about what different foods do, which is really fascinating.

We also do at least one trip a year together—to the Las Vegas Marathon—to promote the Tucson Marathon. Some years we do a second trip, to the Rock 'n' Roll Marathon in San Diego.

I love to go gambling with Pam when we're in Las Vegas. She's amazingly good, and Jim is all for it since Pam usually brings home money. We play roulette. Pam taught me her method: You play several things where you have small odds, like 2:1. So you won't win big, but you usually don't lose your money and you can play for longer. Then you also put one or two chips in higher-risk categories. Pam's also good at blackjack.

I remember one time I was playing keno and Pam came by the table. She was tired and said she didn't feel like playing. She just wanted to go to the sauna or back to her room to lie down. I talked her into playing one round. So she said okay, and she played her kids' birthdays. She won. She took $140 and went up to her room.

—*Elisa Kinder*

I met Susy more than 17 years ago, when I was first getting into running. Susy has a full-time career as an attorney and a judge. She has been married, but she's single right now, and she does not have children. Recently she completed two Ironman Triathlons—the Hawaiian and, 3 weeks later, the Florida—just before going to San Diego with me for the One-Day Race. (She's getting more and more like me all the time! Florida was her best time ever.) I do more traveling to events with Susy than with anyone else, whether she's crewing for me (she's done all four Badwaters) or we're both competing in an event. As my "single" friend, she's more flexible. I don't know what I would do without her.

When we run together, usually we aren't about speed, unless one of us has a particular goal for an event that's coming up. Generally, we are just very relaxed and go along at whatever pace suits us, talking about different races. Sometimes I tell her the latest crazy thing that's going on with the marathon, or we talk about her work—from convicts to DUIs. Susy has told me about how perps can be really horrible (I guess this is no surprise) and sometimes even spit on her. She carries antibacterial gel to wash up with after she sees them. Susy is one of only two women who serve as judge at her level in Tucson. She acts like this is no big deal.

Rhina, who has run almost 30 marathons, is married to Rich Gerhauser, the Tucson Marathon's medical director and a hugely talented bike racer. I think he could have been a major competitor if he'd had the time to devote to the sport. Like me, Rhina has three boys, so we often talk about our parenting issues and techniques or, in my case, the lack thereof. Unlike me, Rhina is very, very hands-on with her kids, which gives me a different perspective.

Once Rhina and I were talking with another friend about how much time you have to invest to be a serious runner. Our friend, who is a Catholic, had been advised by her priest to give up running because he thought it must have been taking time away from her family. Our friend told him that she ran at five in the morning just to prevent that. The priest countered that running still could be a problem since getting up at five was probably making her tired. Rhina mentioned that she hears this same accusation from women who go out for 2-hour lunches, including cocktails. Some people seem to feel that running is somehow self-indulgent and makes you a bad parent.

I've known Patty since Jim and I bought our first house in Jackson. The woman who had owned the house introduced us. She and Patty were running partners. Patty and I have been running together ever since, which means that Patty knows pretty much everything about me that there is to know. She was a competitive swimmer in college, and we sometimes swim together too. But it's hard to talk and swim at the same time! Her husband, whom she met at a wedding in Minnesota, is from an old Jackson Hole family, so that's where she ended up living. She's very connected to the community and we talk about that, along with exchanging the usual stories about our husbands or kids. We usually run on her land, which is located right on the Snake River. It's gorgeous there. I know people who would give an arm or leg for that land. It's a pleasure to run there.

It's funny that all of my running partners are women now. Except for doing an occasional event together, Jim and I don't run together that much anymore. Maybe running with women is the flip side of living in a nearly all-male household. Women traveling together to do running events, like little vacations, also seems to be a trend— they just take off to do a marathon or an Ironman together. I see this primarily among boomer women, but with a lot of younger ones, too. It'll be neat to see if this trend continues.

Although running is a big part of my life, with my girlfriends it's really just an excuse to be together. We run in the morning instead of eating breakfast. We run at noon. We run at night. We never get bored. And we never shut up.

CHAPTER 31

WHERE WOMEN
CAN WIN

Ultrarunning is one of the few sports in which women and men compete directly against each other. Usually it's men against men and women against women. There are also a few events in which only one gender competes, like the balance beam in gymnastics. Throughout society, the number of exclusively male sports has definitely been decreasing. There are now female boxers, wrestlers, and even a few high school and college football players. But only in ultrarunning do women—as individuals, rather than team members—compete directly against men on the same course, at the same time, under the same conditions. Ultrarunning doesn't even recognize age groups, which is of particular importance. In other races, even though runners may say that they are competing against themselves, there is still a sense that women are in competition with other women but not with men, and that older runners are not competing with younger people. For instance, during triathlons, each participant's age is written on the back of his or her calf, and if I see a 29-year-old pass me, I'm not going to be concerned, because I'm in the 45-to-49 category. Ultrarunners, however, race against the entire field. When you're used to making judgments about who you should or shouldn't be able to beat, competing against young and old alike opens up your mind to doing your best without limiting your expectations.

Occasionally, women are even the overall winners of ultrarunning events. If the sport becomes more popular, this will probably happen more often. I think this could be very important for reasons I'll discuss in a moment. First I'd like to tell you some of the reasons I think women can do especially well in ultra events.

In 1992, the prestigious science journal *Nature* published an article entitled "Will Women Soon Outrun Men?" The authors were two UCLA researchers, Brian Whipp and Susan Ward, who had studied world-record running speeds at various distances for men and women, going back to the beginning of the 20th century. They found that at distances from 200 meters up to 10 kilometers, women's times had been improving at a steadily faster rate than men's. At longer distances, such as marathons and beyond, the rate of women's improvement as compared to men's was even greater. Female marathoners, for example, were improving their results four times faster than their male counterparts.

Obviously, if this trend were to continue, the women eventually would surpass the men in terms of record-setting times. The UCLA researchers predicted that the best times for men's and women's marathons would equalize around 1998, with times for other distances also equalizing by the middle of the 21st century.

So far, though, it hasn't happened. At this writing, the UCLA study is almost 15 years old, the "transition year" of 1998 is long past, and none of the predictions has come true. In fact, by 1997, another study showed that the rate of female runners' improvement had leveled off and even fallen behind that of men. According to the authors of this second study, Steven Sailer and Stephen Seiler, women not only were failing to do better compared to men but also were doing consistently worse. To explain these findings, the authors did not contradict the earlier research. Instead, they introduced a variable that, in their opinion, had been previously overlooked: the influence of performance-enhancing chemicals. Sailer and Seiler asserted that the dramatic improvement in women's running times had been caused by the use of steroids and other drugs. Similarly, the drop-off in women's performance was caused by the introduction of strict and improved drug testing. Of course, if women were benefiting from drugs, men were probably taking them too. Sailer and Seiler presented evidence that steroids affect females more dramatically than they do males, so the changes in women's performance were likely to be greater. The overall message of the study was that men's performance superiority will continue as long as drugs are effectively supervised.

Both studies looked closely at trends in athletes' performance and drew careful statistical conclusions. In the end, they canceled each other out. If women's performances had been improving and drugs were the cause of the improvement, let's look at settings in which no drugs are available. Kenya, for instance, has produced many great distance runners over the years, and no drugs have been available. As a rule, Kenyan male athletes have had greater success than Kenyan women. This was, at least in part, a result of differences in their training: The Kenyan men simply trained more effectively. Theirs was a tradition of men training in groups and of young runners being mentored by older, highly successful athletes. Kenyan women have been more isolated in their training. Mentoring among female athletes has been rare. Also, there simply have been a greater number of male athletes. With a higher percentage of the male population taking part in sports, there's a greater chance for the best male athletes to emerge.

Many of these factors also affect American athletes, especially in sports like ultrarunning that aren't included in heavily publicized (and subsidized) events like the Olympic Games. An American woman who isn't an Olympic athlete but who really devotes herself to running is likely to be seen as eccentric, to put it kindly. A man is just seen as someone who's devoted to running. Even women themselves can sometimes feel this way.

I consider this to be really unfortunate. I believe that women have a superior aptitude for certain sports, including ultrarunning. If women could free themselves from the negativity that has affected both their physical training and their emotional connection to their sport, I think we would see women doing really well in ultrarunning. As a result, more women would take up the sport. Part of the reason I'm writing this book is to help that process along.

I'm not saying any of this as an outsider. I've described my frustration with what I perceived to be a lack of commitment by the other women on my college tennis team. I know that even then there were female athletes who were just as devoted to sports as I was, so maybe I just went to the wrong college. But 25 years ago, it wasn't cool for a woman to be too serious about sports. This is definitely changing, so that female soccer, volleyball, or basketball players are now able to get as deeply into their sports as men are. In a sport like ultrarunning, however, women are still pretty much on their own—which is an interesting paradox, since ultrarunning is probably the one sport in which women really can be the best in the world.

This doesn't mean I'm hoping for a female Michael Jordan—someone who will get her face on a cereal box or start a line of clothing. In fact, I think market-driven adulation of celebrity athletes can be a dangerous thing in many ways. "Be like Mike" was a clever advertising tagline that translated into a generation of playground ballplayers trying to build their games around shots that Michael made once in his life.

What I really hope to see is not just a few stars being admired but rather the *participation* of large numbers of women in sports like ultrarunning, where they really can excel.

CONCLUSION:
ACCOMPLISHMENTS

When I look back at my career so far, some races really stand out in terms of how they made me feel afterward. I want to mention a few of these, and I want to talk a little about accomplishment in general.

First, there was the Ironman Canada that Jim and I trained for and competed in together. As I've already mentioned, my surprisingly strong showing at this race was a total revelation to me. For the first time I had the sense of having real potential, of being someone who could be, as Marlon Brando said in *On the Waterfront*, a contender. Jim had believed in me, and after that race I believed in myself.

The second milestone was a race that I decided to run at the last minute. In the Prologue to this book, I described my own weekend-long version of an ultra race across the country that concluded with my running in the 100th Boston Marathon. The first leg of that ultra, the Mule Mountain Marathon, was the very first race in which I placed first among women. At the time, I barely had a moment to think about it, but it was really meaningful to me. Jim actually took the T-shirt from that race and framed it for me. I usually don't care about race souvenirs—I have all kinds of race bling and buckles. (The ones from Leadville are huge—they cover my whole belly!) But this shirt and a photo of me from my first Badwater that Jim had blown up and framed are really cherished mementos.

For a long time after the failure of the travel agency that my mother had bought, I felt that I just wasn't a good person. I didn't feel that I was of use to anyone. I'd been a business major, and I couldn't even run a business. In spite of my increasing success in running, in important ways I didn't think I had anything to offer. My self-esteem was very low. It's not exaggerating to say that at times I actually felt that my kids would be better off without me. Again, it was Jim who eventually gave me some idea of what I could do. Taking on the Tucson Marathon changed my life. It was something I could put my whole heart and soul into. I'm really proud of what Pat and Elisa and I (along with Mary Croft and her volunteers) accomplished. We created a business that is a success.

And it *is* my business, my work. Sometimes people ask me, "What charity is this for? Who does it benefit?" I want to say, "*You*. You are running for your health. It benefits *you*."

For the past few years, I've felt like I've been at a crossroads with the marathon. It is time-consuming and fraught with unforeseen disasters that keep me stressed for months of the year. And there are other things I want to do. Also, my family may be moving more permanently to Wyoming. I have tried to sell the business a couple of times but then had second thoughts. It's hard to let it go. It's meant so much to me.

The fourth milestone for me was winning Badwater. Truthfully, I never expected that. The feeling I had after that race is almost indescribable. It was just a total sense of peace.

I'd talked with my sister, Debbie, about my inability to be "in the moment" in my life. She claimed that she often felt like everything was okay just as it was—something I could not even imagine. If I was swimming, I'd be thinking about when I could go running. If I was shopping, I'd be mentally running through points for an upcoming meeting. Whatever was going on was never enough. I usually would be very critical of myself, focus on my flaws. After Badwater, I finally knew what Debbie was talking about. I was so elated, and the feeling spilled into every aspect of my life. I walked around in love with everything. Everything was okay exactly as it was.

Eventually, of course, the feeling of total peace went away, especially when I began to hear that people were saying my win had been a fluke. For a while, though, it was fantastic. I wish I could have bottled it.

My fourth time at Badwater was another big one for me. I had won for the second time in '03, and then lost in '04. In 2005, I really didn't want to do Badwater again. Truthfully, I was scared to put myself out there. I'd had a very mixed year and hadn't done as well as I'd have liked to in a number of races. I'd probably also done too many races during that spring and early summer. Plus, there had been all of that hoopla about the supposed rivalry between Dean Karnazes and me. I was also starting to notice that it bothered me more when other runners passed me. It made me feel a little like I was losing it. So my big accomplishment at Badwater '05 was that I got myself to the starting line. After that, whatever happened was okay.

The last big one at the time of this writing was the 2005 San Diego One-Day Race. I'd won the U.S. women's division American National 24-Hour Run Championship 2 years earlier, and I went there with the goal of winning it again. What made this race so memorable and gave me the greatest sense of accomplishment was how hard I had to fight for it. When something's easy, I never feel really satisfied. But if I try really hard, even if I don't win, I still feel good about it. Everybody needs that, maybe even more so as we get older and begin to let go of the satisfactions and sense of identity that we get from our jobs.

I think we tend to underestimate our own abilities at all levels. I think of the speech that Ken Chlouber, the race director, gives at the start of the Leadville Trail 100. He says, "You are better than you think you are, and you can do more than you think you can."

(I always try to remember that when I am in the middle of the race and feel like crap.)

It's something that all of us should try to keep in mind. Susy, for instance, is just killer. She's *way* better than she gives herself credit for. Another friend, Diane, is a 52-year-old massage therapist and a distance swimmer. She thinks of herself as a triathlete but doesn't give herself any credit as a runner. Five years ago she took a sabbatical from everything because of a heart problem. Then she went to Brazil to do an Ironman and did it 1½ hours faster than she'd done it before! She'd never do a marathon because she'd get upset when she was passed. We had to practically force her to do a 10-miler, and then she ended up taking fourth place in a field of 26!

My literary agent's story is another case in point. The only sport she'd ever done was a season of junior varsity field hockey when she was a sophomore in high school. She liked to run, but her school didn't have a girls' track team. So she would do laps with the boys' team. They eventually made her scorekeeper for their meets. She only did that for 1 year. Then for 30 years she did no exercise at all except for walking to do errands in New York City, where she lives. When she received the proposal for this book, she began to think, "Well, Pam is only a few years younger than I am." While she could not picture herself running 135 miles across Death Valley, she thought she might be able to do *something*. In the summer of '04, she began running around the reservoir in Central Park. Then she joined the New York Road Runners Club and, that September, did her first 4-mile race. She raced all winter, and by April of '05 she had done enough races—from 5-Ks to half-marathons—to qualify for the ING New York City Marathon in '06. She'll be 49 when she runs it.

We're not all top runners. It's all in our minds. Given the age of many runners today, I can honestly say that at age 45 I may be only beginning the second half of my career. Even though it might not seem this way when we're actually in a race, time is on our side. For older runners, the longer the race, the better. We've got patience.

There's one last thing that I want to bring up in conclusion— leave it to me to finish with a gripe. Or, actually, a gripe and a suggestion for a change I'd like to see occur.

One thing that always bugs me is when I see race directors for U.S. marathons or other long races paying non-American runners to come over and compete. U.S. distance runners are not that competitive on the world level, so frequently Ethiopians or Kenyans are brought over as guests. This is essentially importing the favorites. The runners' transportation costs are paid, as are their hotel bills and sometimes even appearance fees. I'm not sure why this is. Is it to attract an audience? To set a faster pace? To give U.S. runners (or other paid entrants) someone to try to beat? It doesn't make sense to me. Usually, the guest runners take the prize on top of having all of their expenses paid. This outcome is pretty much expected, so with rare exceptions there is little incentive for American runners.

To me this is a symptom, if not part of the cause, of something very sad that I see when I compete internationally with an American team. In distance running, for the most part, Americans are distinct individuals. They are not a team. They do not have uniforms, they do not have funding, they do not have a coach. It's every woman or man for her- or himself, usually including finding a way to get to the event. Other countries have more team camaraderie. A lot of them have uniforms. They are coached. They give off the sense of being "together." Even the team members from some of the very poor countries, though they are not well dressed, have a more unified vibe than we do.

I think about this a lot, and I'm not sure why it is. Here in America we are so cutthroat with each other. There's so little support here that we fight for crumbs like a dysfunctional family.

In America, such a rich country, why are there only crumbs? It doesn't make any sense.

This may be a new project for me, trying to find some way to make Team America more of a team. Those of us who really love distance running should not be undercutting each other, but rather building a strong support system together. I know money isn't the answer to every problem. But finding or raising some funding that would allow our top racers to get where they need to go could open doors for talent we don't even know about, as well as take care of the established elite runners who now compete on their own dime while representing their country.

If I could pull off something like that, just think of the sense of accomplishment it would bring.

EPILOGUE:
A WEEK AND A HALF
OF RIDICULOUS

The year I turned 40, Jim and I, along with two of our boys, Tim and Greg, had planned a trip to climb Wyoming's Grand Teton at the end of July. It was a package trip, all paid for, and we were looking forward to it with a lot of excitement. As usual, the days and weeks leading up to that getaway were packed with running dates.

On July 20, I ran the Elkhorn 100-K in Helena, Montana, with Jim crewing. I'd run this race a number of times and done well, winning several times. It's a race that I usually enjoy. This particular time I had some trouble. For a stretch around mile 20, the course is a very rocky single-track trail. I rarely fall, but this time I did. And the moment I did I realized that I had probably broken my right hand. I was familiar with the course, so I knew that there was an aid station about 3 miles farther on. I didn't have any choice but to keep going at least to that point. I figured that once I got there, I'd see what the medical staff said and decide whether or not to keep going.

As I ran, my hand didn't really bother me that much. Other than hurting like crazy when I tipped up my water bottle, it seemed fine. I knew that the trail was so remote that from the aid station at mile 25 it would probably take 4 hours for anyone to get me out of there. The thought of sitting around waiting was so unappealing that I decided I might as well just go ahead and finish the race. So when I got to the aid station I just told them that I had fallen, not mentioning that my hand was most likely broken.

When I saw Jim waiting for me at around mile 50, I told him what had happened and that I wanted to finish and go to the doctor afterward. That became the plan. I ended up coming in first woman, and I think third overall. At the finish, a doctor looked at my hand, agreed that it was broken, and sent us to a little emergency room about 7 miles away.

It was late Saturday afternoon and, unlike some other emergency room experiences I've had, this one went pretty quickly. The x-ray showed a small break in the bone by the little finger. The doctor recommended waiting 3 or 4 days before getting it set, to let the swelling go down. He made a temporary cast with an elastic bandage and a white square of something that shaped itself to my hand and set quickly. Jim and I spent the night in Helena and then went home on Sunday.

I had planned a trail run with a friend on Monday. I didn't feel like canceling—I had confidence in my little cast—so off I went for a nice 8- or 9-mile jaunt before driving myself to Salt Lake City for the marathon that was to be held the next day. I got sort of a late start and barely made it to registration after calling ahead to let them know I was on my way. That night I went to bed, got up, and ran the race, winning the masters group and the prize of $500. Then I drove back to Jackson Hole.

Wednesday I went to see a doctor about my hand. The doctor sent me to a surgeon, who informed me that if I didn't have surgery I would not regain full use of my hand. I scheduled the surgery for Thursday morning.

The surgeon was really good. After he had done his work, he didn't think I needed a cast. He probably had no idea of the kind of constant activity I'm used to—or maybe he thought common sense would make me take it easy. Let's just say he might have given me too much credit. Later that day, Jim reminded me about the Snow King Hill Climb scheduled for that afternoon. Snow King is a *smoking* hill climb, an annual local event where the prize is a ski pass. The race is only 2.3 miles—0.5 of that is flat, then there's a 1.8-mile climb up something like 1,600 feet of Snow King Mountain. I'd won it a couple of times in the past, so with Jim saying, "You can't miss this!" we headed off to do it. I was not the winner that day and finished as the fourth woman. For some reason I was having chest pain—maybe from the anesthesia. It hurt enough to be scary.

The next day, Friday, I went on another previously scheduled trail run with a woman friend. We'd planned to go 18 miles, 9 up a mountain and 9 back down. Again, though, I got chest pains. They were really extreme, and I was annoyed that I could not keep up.

On Saturday we had to start practicing for the scheduled climb of Grand Teton. Of course, the surgeon had told me that I was not allowed to climb. And at first, the practice instructor was pretty skeptical that I'd be able to do it. He said that if I couldn't manage to his satisfaction over the weekend, I wouldn't be able to climb on Monday. I was not about to forgo the climb. I had kept the cute little cast that had been put on in the emergency room in Helena, so I fastened that around my hand again with an elastic bandage. I could use my left hand and the fingers sticking out of the cast on my right. After 2 days of practice, I managed to qualify for the mountain climb.

We set out at around 8:00 or 9:00 a.m. Monday morning and climbed to base camp. The next morning we rose at 2:00 or 3:00 a.m. to give ourselves enough time to summit the 13,770-foot peak and still get back down the mountain before dark.

Call me irresponsible, but I had a wonderful time. Those 10 crazy days were in some ways pretty typical back then. I think that these days I'm a little more of a wimp. I definitely rest more.

PAM REED'S
CAREER HIGHLIGHTS
AND RECORDS

Overall winner of Badwater Ultramarathon: 2002 and 2003

Women's record holder for Badwater Ultramarathon: 27 hours, 56 minutes (2002)

24-Hour American Women's record on a track: 138.96 miles (2003)

48-Hour American Women's Age Group (40 to 44) record: 212 miles (2004)

Women's National Champion of San Diego One-Day Race: 134.56 miles (2005)

First woman (as far as we know) to run 300 miles with no sleep: 2005

Transatlantic triple marathon (London/double Boston): less than 48 hours (2005)

Pam Reed has run more than 100 marathons (her personal record is 2:59, set in 2001) and more than 100 ultramarathons. In 1999, she ran a grand slam (four 100-mile races). She has run the Wasatch Front 100 ten times.

AWARDS AND HONORS

2003 USA Track & Field Women's Masters Ultrarunner of the Year

2003 *Competitor* magazine Endurance Sports Athlete of the Year

Arizona Daily Star 2003 Top 100 Sports Figures in Arizona: Number 3

Arizona Daily Star 2005 Top 100 Sports Figures in Arizona: Number 9

ACKNOWLEDGMENTS

In the process of telling all of my stories, I realized just how many amazing friends I have. So many people helped me with this book, and so many more have been there for me in my life. It's not possible to thank everyone I'd like to, but I'll give it a try.

First, I want to thank Chuck Giles. If not for Chuck, I don't think I'd have a story interesting enough to warrant a book. It was Chuck's vision that turned a sport I was passionate about into my career. I can't thank him enough for that.

Thanks to my agent, Stephany Evans. She is amazing. I have never met anyone more dedicated and hardworking. She's the reason the book was even finished.

A big thank-you to Elisa Kinder for all of her help and friendship through the years. She is the most positive person I know. I thank Susy Bacal for being such a great friend and running partner. She is never in a bad mood. She listens to me complain all the time. She is one of the smartest and nicest people I know. Linda Brewer deserves thanks for being there in really hard times. She stayed out for 2 of the 3 nights of the 300-miler, and she also traveled to France to help me with the 48-hour race.

Another big thank-you goes to my mom and dad, Karen and Roy Saari, for putting up with me. I'm not the "loving daughter" type, but they are always there when I need them. Also, thanks to Debbie Wickstrom, my sister. She never has a bad thing to say about anyone. She is very content in her life—I strive for that.

Thank you to Benny Linkhart for being a no-strings-attached

kind of friend. When I call him it is as if we have been talking every day, even when it has been more than a year. Thanks also for motivating me when I'd just started doing the long runs.

Craig Bellmann—this guy didn't even know me and yet he turned up for Badwater twice. He has a great heart and soul. He has really great energy. To Diane Dedeck, massage therapist and Tucson friend: I'm so glad we met. You have given me so much to think about and lots of positive vibes. My friend Rhina Gerhauser is such a good person and mother. We have run together for many hours, talking about our kids, figuring out life. And to Rich Gerhauser, thanks for finally getting me to take my vitamins and amino acids— I feel *terrific!*

My neighbor Gail Rowland is so amazing—she's a single mom with two adopted kids. We talk at the bus stop. She's so smart; she has great wisdom and insight. Mary Croft is one of the coolest people I know. At 60, she never stops going and traveling. She is also tremendously generous with her time, a virtue that is hard for me to practice and that I really admire. Patty Gill, my steady Jackson running buddy and mom extraordinaire, is always good for a creative idea on the parenting front.

A really huge thank-you to all of those who gave their blood, sweat, and tears to crew for me, especially at Badwater and the 300-miler: Chuck, Susy, Craig, Scott Scheff, Carol Trevey, Lee Moore, Jeff Balmat, Doug Kelly, Stephanie Pearmain, Dave and Michelle Hill, Colleen and Mike, Timothy Koski, Roy Saari, Bob Wolfe, Bev Schultz, Stacy Weisner, and Pastor John Wall, who ran with me on Easter Day.

Thank you to Charlie Engle for his incredible *enthusiasm*. I'm looking forward to sharing more adventures in the future!

I need to thank Mike Kasser, whose company, Holualoa, is the biggest sponsor of the Tucson Marathon and who has supported me personally as an athlete as well. A very big thank-you to you, Mike!

A special thank-you to my sponsors, Red Bull, Recover-Ease, Wickie Wear, Coolmax, and PowerSox, who also have supported my career (and this book!), and to Amino Vital, one of my earliest sponsors. And to all the other sponsors who keep the Tucson Marathon going: Desert Diamond Casino, PODS, VitaminWater, Comp-1, the Hilton Tucson El Conquistador, Aloe Splash, Craig Dahler Jewelers, Clif Shot, Bruegger's Bagels, Oasis Bottled Water, Tucson Water, Fitness Plus, Pepsi, Catalina Mart, Performance Footwear, and the Southern Arizona Roadrunners. A particular thank-you to Jim Click and Jim Click Automotive, who have been with us since the very beginning. Thank you, too, to Lute Olson (the University of Arizona's head basketball coach) and Heather Alberts of Better Than Ever for allowing us to cooperate with them in raising money for ovarian cancer in Bobbi's memory.

My publisher, Rodale, has been amazing. So many people there have given their talents to make this a good book, and I thank them all. I especially want to thank Leah Flickinger, who signed me up and got me to the starting line, and Kathy LeSage, who has been crew chief extraordinaire on my first publishing ultramarathon. Bet you wondered if we'd ever see the finish line, huh, Kathy?

My appreciation to Bob Yehling for getting the whole book thing started and to Mitch Sisskind for giving it shape and talking me into doing my fourth Badwater.

If I have forgotten anyone, please know that I do appreciate your friendship and contribution in my life. You know how I am. I almost forgot to thank *Chuck*, if you can believe that!

I really want to say how blessed my life is. I have my health and am able to do all the cool things that I enjoy. I have a great family and great friends. I am the luckiest person I know.

Finally, thanks again to Jim. I love you!